Battlecry

Winning the battle for the mind
with a slogan that kills

LAURA RIES

ALSO BY LAURA RIES

Visual Hammer

BOOKS BY AL & LAURA RIES

Focus: The Future of Your Company Depends on It

The 22 Immutable Laws of Branding

The 11 Immutable Laws of Internet Branding

The Fall of Advertising & the Rise of PR

The Origin of Brands

War in the Boardroom

Visit Ries.com for more information.

Battlecry

Dedicated to Brendan Brown,
my second son with the alliterative name.

CONTENTS

Ries & Ries, 1994

PREFACE
BY AL RIES

I've given hundreds of marketing speeches in 60 different countries around the world. After my speeches are over, I usually answer questions from people in the audience and later from media reporters. Now, what do you think is the No.1 question I've been asked?

How did you get your daughter Laura to work with you?

The answer is, I didn't. She decided she wanted to work with me. In retrospect, I should have known that was true.

In high school, Laura took an unusual interest in selling her ideas. When she had to deliver a presentation to her class, she would make elaborate flip charts to illustrate the major points of her speech.

Like the dozens of 35mm slides she put together for a presentation about the life of Shakespeare.

When the time came to choose a college, she picked Northwestern, perhaps the school with the nation's best reputation for marketing. After graduating from Northwestern in 1993 "with highest honors," she worked as an account executive for TBWA, a New York City advertising agency,

In 1994, she joined me to start Ries & Ries, a marketing firm in Great Neck, New York. In 1997, we relocated to Atlanta, Georgia.

Advertising agencies have an advantage that marketing-strategy firms do not. They can promote themselves by publicizing the advertisements they do for their clients. (Clients expect their agencies do this.)

Early on, I learned marketing firms don't have that same advantage. Burger King fired us because I was foolish enough to tell a magazine about one of their ideas we were working on.

So how can a marketing-strategy firm promote itself? Two ways: Books and speeches.

Actually, the two work together. The books drive the speeches. The speeches drive the consulting business.

Since we started our marketing-strategy firm, Laura and I wrote five marketing books together.

Our key book is the first one we published. *Focus: The Future of Your Company Depends on It.*

Without a focus, it's difficult to build a brand with any of the other strategies we have devised.

That's why we call our marketing firm, *Focusing consultants.*

Most marketing consultants have no coherent strategy themselves. They are perfectly willing to tell you what to do, but they seldom take their own advice. We do.

We help our consulting clients refocus their companies around a singular idea or concept.

If you study successful companies, they initially built their brands with a single conceptual idea.

Dell . . . . *Personal computers sold direct to businesses.*

Zappos . . *Free shipping, both ways.*

FedEx . . *Overnight delivery.*

Over time, companies drift sideways. They get into many different businesses and often lose their focus.

Much of the work we do is to help companies develop strategies to recapture their initial momentum.

This often requires going back to basics and verbalizing a brand's key concept in a memorable slogan.

The slogan has two major functions: (1) It re-establishes the brand in consumers' minds, and (2) It keeps the company's marketing people from changing the company's strategy.

How do you develop a slogan that can effectively position a brand in your prospect's mind?

There are five different verbal techniques to accomplish this task. Laura will describe each of them in detail.

Each of these five techniques can greatly increase the memorability of a marketing slogan.

And memorability is the key to effectiveness. The perfect slogan (from the company's point of view) is useless if nobody remembers it or associates it with the company's brand.

You might be surprised by some of the techniques Laura has devised to turn an ordinary slogan into an effective *Battlecry*.

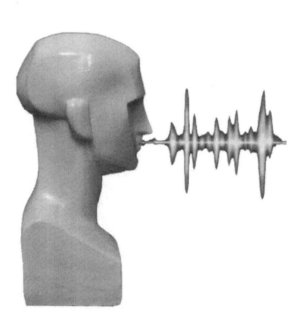

Chapter 1

WORDS VS. SOUNDS

We live in a world of words. The average person spends two hours a day reading and answering email.

Then there's Google. And Facebook. And Twitter. And other sites that attract our attention. More words, words, words.

If you want to remember something, goes the saying, write it down. That's why we make up "to-do" lists. And shopping lists. And recipes. More words, words, words.

People think words are the only way of communicating an idea.

The media we respect are the ones that deal with words.

Rated even higher on "respect" than national newspapers and magazines, are non-fiction books.

It's difficult to become a top

The New York Times

Los Angeles Times

The Washington Post

THE WALL STREET JOURNAL.

professor at a leading university in America without writing a few books. Whether they become best-sellers or not.

As far as radio and television is concerned, we tend to think of them as "entertainment" media. Not good enough to make the big time.

Printed words reign supreme. Spoken words are considered inferior to printed text. They're just someone's interpretation of the real thing.

But in reality it's exactly the opposite. Spoken sounds are primary. Printed words are just physical representations of spoken sounds.

Say "O," for example, and you will notice that your lips form a circle. The other letters of the alphabet also have their origins in how sounds were formed in the mouth.

Not only are printed words secondary to spoken sounds, but also words themselves are not the way your mind thinks.

Your mind can't understand words. It can only understand sounds. Therefore, a printed word must first be translated into a sound before your mind can understand it.

A sound can be understood almost immediately, but it takes time for a printed word to be understood. There's a reason for this delay.

A mind consists of two brains: a left brain which handles sounds, a right brain which handles visuals.

A printed word is a visual.

(2) Then sent to left brain and transformed into sound.

(1) It enters right brain to be decoded.

A printed word is a visual that enters your mind in the right brain where it is decoded and then sent to your left brain where it is transformed into sound. That takes time, approximately 40 milliseconds.

It doesn't sound like much, but if our stoplights were verbal instead of visual, you could expect even more carnage on our highways.

Instead, our stoplights are visual with red for *stop,* green for *go* and yellow for *caution.*

The visual half of your mind, the right brain, recognizes symbols without needing verbal translations. That's why you can react quickly when a stoplight changes color.

That's why touch typing is much faster than "hunt and peck." A touch typist uses only his or her right brain to operate a keyboard.

Touch typists "visually know" where the letters on a keyboard are, but verbally cannot tell you because that activity involves the left brain.

"Hunt and peck" typists first need to learn where each letter is, an activity organized in the left brain. Then when typing, they translate that information letter by letter to the right brain where the visual function of operating a keyboard is carried out.

Watch a child learning how to read. You'll notice the child moving his or her lips. Why is that? Because the child is translating the visual images of type into sounds he or she can understand.

Grown-ups don't move their lips, but they still convert printed words (in reality the visual images) into sounds before they can be understood.

Note the confusion that exists between words like *there* and *their*. And between words like *compliment* and *complement*.

Even though the spelling of each of the two words is different, the sounds are similar, hence the confusion.

There is no confusion, however, between two similar words like *dessert* and *desert* because they are pronounced differently.

Dessert. **Desert.**

It's the sounds that differentiate the two words, not the spelling.

(Some people don't know which spelling is the sweet treat and which spelling is the sand dunes.)

Ten percent of menus posted by restaurants on the GrubHub.com website misspell the word *dessert*.

But do companies recognize the critical importance of "sounds" in the formulation of their advertising messages?

Apparently not.

In the Buckhead section of Atlanta, there's an apartment complex with hundreds of units.

The name? *Elle.*

Looks like a very good name. After all, *Elle* is also the name of a best-selling fashion magazine.

But put yourself in the place of an Elle tenant who meets someone who asks, "Where do you live?"

I live in Elle.

Sorry to hear you're living in hell. I know the economy is bad, but I didn't realize things were that bad.

No, I mean the Elle apartments. E . . L . . L . . E.

It might not be obvious, but companies can make the same mistake. A company will evaluate potential brand names by writing them on flip charts or presenting them in PowerPoint slides.

Or distributing them in memos or emails. All in print, of course.

Managers are so used to working in print that they seldom consider the sound a brand name or a slogan might convey.

Consider *ShopHouse,* a new Southeast-Asian fast-casual food chain being developed by Chipotle Mexican Grill, one of the most-successful restaurant operators.

ShopHouse? The name looks right, but when a consumer says the name, it sounds something like *SlopHouse.*

Not a good connotation for a restaurant chain. You can imagine a review by an unhappy customer: *ShopHouse is a SlopHouse.*

Once a potential customer hears the words together, *ShopHouse* and *SlopHouse,* it makes an emotional connection.

And once an emotional connection is made between those words, it's almost impossible to forget them.

There's there Lite, a beer brand introduced by Miller Brewing Co. Lite became an instant success, revolutionizing the beer category.

Today, light beer accounts for more than 65 percent of beer sold in America.

In print, Lite beer is easily distinguished from Bud Light, Coors Light and dozens of other beers. But one of the biggest beer-distribution channels is bars and taverns.

Give me a Lite beer, a customer might ask the bartender.

What kind of light beer do you want? the bartender might reply.

In the mind, *Lite* sounds just like *light.* (In the mind, there are no capital or lower-case letters.)

Eventually Miller Brewing recognized its naming mistake and added the *Miller* name to its *Lite* beer. But the brand never recovered from its initial naming error and today trails both Bud Light and Coors Light.

Kmart recently took advantage of the confusion factor that can exist between words and sounds.

An online Kmart video promoted a new program that lets customers ship items they can't find in the store to their homes for free.

In the video, a Kmart employee explains the free-shipping policy to an incredulous customer.

The first week it was released, the video received 12 million views and Kmart began airing it on TV.

The next video from Kmart also used words in a way that made

them sound like expletives. Actors talked about the *big gas savings* they get when fueling up at Kmart.

The brand is in trouble, so it's doubtful if these sophomoric videos will turn Kmart around. But there's no question they have captured the attention of millions of people.

As the Kmart videos demonstrate, it's not words that give meaning to a name or a slogan. It's the sounds that convey the meanings.

In truth, people don't talk in the sounds of words at all. They talk in the sounds of syllables.

Let's-go-to-the-mo-vies-to-night.

Computer programs that turn words into sounds are often difficult to understand because they lack three characteristics of spoken words: Pitch, loudness and emphasis.

Except for "pitch," one could visualize how the above sentence might actually be delivered.

*Let's-go-to-the . . . **mov-ies** . . . to-night.*

The response might be delivered the following way.

*Let-go-to-the-mov-ies . . . **to-mor-row** night.*

You probably have noticed that the words *motion pictures* are used frequently in news stories. But consumers invariably say *movies* instead of *motion pictures.*

Mov-ies are two syllables and *mo-tion pic-tures* are four syllables. When given a choice, consumers will almost always use the shorter not the longer version.

Most people say *cop.* Not *law-enforcement officer.*

The same principle applies to slogans. Company executives usually like the formality of words like *motion pictures,* but slogans are more effective when colloquial expressions like *movies* are used.

The long-lasting Nike slogan is memorable because it reflects the way people talk. "Quit complaining. *Just do it.*"

Pitch alone can sometimes be used to create a memorable slogan. For example, women usually have higher-pitch voices than men.

But not always.

Starting in 1984, Wendy's ran a series of television commercials featuring three older women being served an enormous bun with a minuscule hamburger patty inside.

While two of the women admire the big bun, the third woman (Clara Peller) gets on the phone with customer service and yells, *Where's the beef?*

What made the commercial memorable was Clara Peller's loud, gravelly voice, coming from a small, elderly woman. It was shocking because it was so unexpected.

In 1984, more than 24,000 consumers were asked to name the year's most-outstanding advertising campaign. The No.1 campaign: Wendy's.

Sales that year went up 26 percent.

Walter Mondale used the line *Where's the beef* against Gary Hart in his successful bid for the 1984 Democratic presidential nomination. Newsweek featured the two politicians on its cover with the headline: *Showdown. Who's got the beef?*

Company management was ecstatic. One executive said, "With Clara, we accomplished as much in five weeks as we did in 14 ½ years."

For millions of small companies, TV is not an affordable option. But these examples should help convince small-company management to consider not just the words, but the sounds of the words they use. Even if those words are just used in print media.

Effective slogans are constructed by considering both the meanings of the words and their "sounds." Especially their sounds.

In this Battlecry book, you will learn how to use five techniques to increase the memorability of your advertising slogan: (1) Rhyme. (2) Alliteration. (3) Repetition. (4) Reversal. (5) Double-entendre.

By now, you might think companies and their advertising agencies would be wise to these techniques. But it's surprising how few slogans actually use any of these memory-building tactics.

In a recent survey of 266 advertising slogans, only 19 slogans used any one of them. And some of the 19 were just plain silly.

For example, EDS used the slogan *Globalize, informationalize and individualize* which rhymes but is virtually meaningless.

(Since changed to *Expertise. Answers. Results.* which makes sense but is not very memorable.)

According to The Wall Street Journal, American companies spent $160 billion on advertising in a recent year.

With that kind of money at stake, you might think more companies would pay more attention to how their advertising works.

But they don't. The industry is awash in ad slogans and taglines that nobody can remember.

And even if they remember the slogans, nobody really believes them. Can you *Open happiness* by opening a Coca-Cola? Does Brown Jordan, a firm you probably never heard of, make *The world's finest furniture?*

Look at the advertising slogans used by the four largest automobile advertisers in America. Do you remember any of these?

Go further. **Find new roads.**

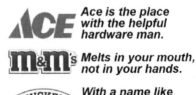

Let's go places. **Start something special.**

Probably not, even though the four companies spend almost $4 billion a year on advertising.

Perhaps it doesn't matter that the slogans aren't memorable. Perhaps the only thing that matters is creating a favorable impression in your mind.

So you might want to mentally jot down the impression each brand has created in your mind.

What's a Ford?

What's a Chevrolet?

What's a Toyota?

What's a Honda?

Not so easy to do, is it? And I wonder if most of your perceptions about these brands were created by articles in the media and not ads?

Or by ownership of one of these brands or by conversations with owners of these brands?

What is the role and function of advertising for well-known brands like Ford and Chevrolet and Toyota and Honda?

It can't be to tell the full story of the brand.

Ford sells 16 different models. Chevrolet sells 18 different models. Most people have trouble just remembering the names of these models, let alone being able to associate the model names with the brand names.

We believe advertising's function is to sum up the essence of a brand in words prospects can remember. (If you can't recall a brand's slogan, you likely weren't affected by the brand's advertising.)

ACE *Ace is the place with the helpful hardware man.*

m&m's *Melts in your mouth, not in your hands.*

SMUCKER'S *With a name like Smucker's, it has to be good.*

And what words do prospects remember? Look at three slogans you might have remembered.

You probably know them all.

20

What's the difference between slogans you remember and those you don't? The memorable slogans have "sounds" that lock the words together in the mind.

Ace is the place . . . uses rhyme to create memorability.

Melts in your mouth . . . uses alliteration to create memorability.

With a name like Smuckers . . . uses reversal to create memorability.

In 1999, Advertising Age, our leading marketing publication, selected the top ten advertising slogans of the 20th century.

How many do you remember? If you're old enough, my guess is you know all ten of these slogans, as well as the names of the brands they stand for.

1. *A diamond is forever.*
2. *Just do it.*
3. *The pause that refreshes.*
4. *Tastes great. Less filling.*
5. *We try harder.*
6. *Good to the last drop.*
7. *Breakfast of champions.*
8. *Does she . . . or doesn't she?*
9. *When it rains, it pours.*
10. *Where's the beef?*

A diamond is forever, the No.1 slogan, is also the oldest. Introduced in 1938, the response to the slogan was almost immediate.

By 1941, diamond sales were up 55 percent.

The De Beers' slogan uses double-entendre to create memorability. A diamond is the hardest substance on earth and should last forever. A diamond ring is the symbol of a love that could last forever, too.

In an era where advertisers tend to change their slogans every year, the longevity of the De Beers slogan is remarkable. It's still used today, even though it's now 77 years old.

Actually, they did take a detour for a couple of years using the slogan *Forever, now* in a retail chain.

In 2001, De Beers entered into a joint venture with Louis Vuitton Moet Hennessy to establish a De Beers retail chain.

The first De Beers boutique opened in London in 2002. Since then, De Beers has opened stores all over the world.

After a few years of *Forever, now*, the chain had the good sense to go back to the original, *A diamond is forever*.

Oddly enough, one thing that can keep a good slogan alive forever are knockoffs and copycats.

Diamonds are forever is the title of Ian Fleming's 1956 novel about the exploits of James Bond.

In 1971, the movie starring Sean Connery was released.

And then there is the 2009 book, *Neil Diamond is forever.* In 2013, BusinessWeek published  a cover story, *Dimon is forever,* recounting the exploits of Jamie Dimon, CEO of JPMorgan Chase.

The De Beers, Ace, M&Ms and Smuckers slogans each illustrate an important principle for creating memorable ideas and concepts.

This book will demonstrate how to use these principles to create memorable slogans for your brands.

High mountain. ? High performance.

Chapter 2

ABSTRACT VS. SPECIFIC

There are two kinds of words. Abstract words and specific words.

Marketing "talk" is loaded with abstract words.

Premium-quality products, customer-oriented sales force, state-of-the-art technology and world-class service.

Many marketing campaigns, especially corporate campaigns, depend almost exclusively on abstractions. That's true of this two-page four-color newspaper advertisement run by Apple.

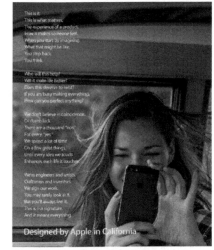

The only specific word in the Apple advertisement is "California." But is California a strong enough reason to prefer Apple products? Aren't most high-tech products designed in California?

I think so.

As you might have expected, the "Designed in California" campaign, which has run on television as well as in newspapers, has been a failure. Bloomberg News called it "a flop with viewers."

Ace Metrix, a firm that analyzes the effectiveness of television ads, reported that the Apple "California" commercial in 2013 earned the lowest score of 27 Apple spots.

Apple, of course, has become an enormously-successful company, the most-valuable company in the world.

But it wasn't because of abstractions like "Designed in California." It was because of tangible ideas linked directly to each of three Apple product introductions: The iPod, iPhone and iPad.

A thousand songs in your pocket.

The first touchscreen smartphone.

Compare Apple with its leading competitors in personal computers: **The first tablet computer.**

Hewlett-Packard, Lenovo and Dell. All three use abstract slogans that could be switched around and nobody would notice.

Make it matter.

Note that all trademarks use the color blue. Not good.

For those who do.

What a slogan and a color should do is to differentiate

Better technology is better business.

your brand from all the other brands in the category.

Apple uses the color "white" which sets it apart from its competitors.

Nor are Apple's three competitors doing well in the marketplace. In the latest year, Hewlett-Packard had a profit margin of 4.5 percent. Dell, 4.2 percent profit margin. And Lenovo, 2.1 percent profit margin. (Apple's profit margin was 21.6 percent.)

The three personal-computer companies aren't the only companies trying to build brands with abstract words. Here are the four slogans used by the leading telecom companies.

AT&T, Verizon, Sprint and T-Mobile. Do you recognize any?

Mobilizing your world. **That's powerful.**

The Un-carrier. **Best value in wireless.**

The four telecom companies have been spending billions of dollars trying to convince you to subscribe to their services.

In 2014, the telecom companies spent $4.2 billion on advertising. (Four of the top 11 advertisers that year were telecom companies.)

Be honest. Do you remember any of their slogans? And furthermore, did any slogan convince you to subscribe to the company's service?

We use AT&T because they are mobilizing our world.

Not a likely consumer response.

To understand why specific words are more effective and memorable than abstract words, you need to consider the two brains in your mind.

The left brain is the logical side of a mind where "thinking" occurs. It operates much like a computer. Logical, analytical, unemotional.

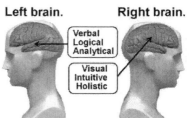

The right brain is the emotional side of a mind. It's also the side that handles "visuals," as well as printed words, the visual symbols that represent sounds. (Your right brain works harder than your left.)

In a manner not totally understood, your right brain will recognize printed symbols for abstract words and send that knowledge to the left brain. Specific words are different.

Like abstract words, your right brain will also recognize printed symbols for specific words and send that information to your left brain.

But specific words like *lake* or *mountain* will also evoke visual images in your right brain.

Since your right brain is also the site of your emotions, specific words have an enormous advantage over abstract words.

They're much more memorable. Think of your own life. What events in your life are the most memorable?

Those events you can visualize. The day you graduated from college. The day you got married. The day you had your automobile accident.

Those visual images will stay with you forever.

Specific words stimulate visual images. The name of your best friend. The make of your automobile. The address of your apartment or home.

Consider some of the world's historic sites: The Great Wall of China, The Eiffel Tower, the Taj Mahal, the Pyramids, the Statute of Liberty.

Just reading the words will evoke visual images of the sites.

Consider some of the world's most-famous people.

Nelson Mandela, Barack Obama, Hillary Clinton, Angelina Jolie, George Clooney, Tiger Woods.

Again, just reading the names will evoke their visual images.

On the other hand, abstract words like *world's historic sites* or *world's most-famous people*

will not conjure up any specific images. Only specific words can do that.

Brand names are also likely to call up visual images in your mind. *Cadillac* evokes images of big cars. *Volkswagen,* small cars.

Brands that don't stay true to their mental images run into trouble. Cadillac's venture into small vehicles like the Cimarron and the Catera were total disasters.

So was Volkswagen's venture into big cars like the Phaeton.

Thousands of business books are published every year by aspiring authors who want to build names for themselves or their companies.

They seldom succeed because they try to look important by using nothing but abstractions.

One example: *How to Think Like a CEO: The 22 Vital Traits You Need to Be the Person at the Top.*

Also, *The CEO, Strategy and Shareholder Value: Making Choices that Maximize Company Performance.*

Sheryl Sandberg used specific words *Lean in* as the title of a book that made her world famous.

Also, she focused on women, not on managers generally.

Not only are abstract words mostly useless in books and marketing, they are also widely

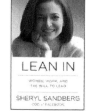

1.6 million books sold.

14,000 Lean-In circles around the world.

overused. Take *innovation*, the current buzzword in corporate circles.

Here is the head and subhead of a Ford corporate advertisement: *Innovation is our mission. The guiding compass of everything we do. Smart, safer, more fuel-efficient vehicles.*

There are only two specific words used in the headline, *vehicles* and *compass* and compass is used out of context.

Ford would have been much better to focus on a specific vehicle to demonstrate the company's commitment to building smarter, safer, more fuel-efficient automobiles.

And look how company executives are using the word *innovation*. Mark Fields, the CEO of Ford, used *innovation* 20 times in a recent keynote address.

Innovation is a highly-abstract concept and also a worn-out word.

In a recent 90-day period, there were 255 books published with *innovation* in their titles.

The word *innovation* was mentioned 33,528 times in a survey of annual and quarterly reports of public companies.

Apple's recent annual report mentioned *innovation* 22 times. And Google's recent annual report mentioned *innovation* 14 times.

(Does that mean Apple is more innovative than Google?)

Twenty-eight percent of business schools use the words *innovation* or *innovative* or *innovate* in their mission statements.

Is innovation important? Sure. "Business has only two functions," wrote Peter Drucker, "Marketing and innovation."

Innovation, like many other abstract words, is both important and useless. Important in business and useless in marketing.

You can often take an abstract idea and make it more memorable by using specific words that create visual images in the mind.

For example, a typical complaint is that Congress is postponing debt reduction until sometime in the future.

Congress is kicking the can down the road says the same thing with specific rather than abstract words.

The words *Kicking the can* call up specific images that "burn" the concept in the mind.

And you probably have noticed that a chief executive never *resigns.* He or she always *steps down.* Specific words create a visual image that makes a resignation more memorable.

A research study conducted by psychology professor Lionel Standing in 1973 demonstrated the memorability of images.

Professor Standing asked his subjects to look at 10,000 images over a five-day period. Each image was presented for just five seconds.

Later, when subjects were shown pairs of images (one they had seen before and one that had not seen), they remembered more than 80 percent of the images they had seen before.

Phenomenal! Try presenting 10,000 slogans for five seconds each and see how many of them people will remember five days later.

If you can create slogans using specific words that conjure up visuals, however, your slogans can last for many generations.

In the early 1970s, our leaders justified military involvement in Vietnam with a simple message.

If the country of Vietnam fell, the entire Southeast Asia region would also fall to communism.

The domino theory.

The domino theory was the visual metaphor to justify the war.

The-most memorable poetry ever written makes extensive use of visual metaphors.

Thomas Gray, 1751: *Full many a flower is born to blush unseen . . and waste its sweetness on the desert air.*

Joyce Kilmer, 1913: *I think that I shall never see . . a poem as lovely as a tree.*

Abstract words are frequently (and ineffectively) used in the names of companies, especially in the names of smaller companies.

Some examples are shown here.

Is Superior Plumbing superior to its competitors?

Saying so doesn't make it so.

And because the Superior name doesn't summon any visual images,

it fails to provide an emotional connection for the Superior brand.

Many brands were built with marketing slogans using specific words. But in an effort to broaden their target markets, companies "generalize" their slogans and turn them into meaningless abstract ideas.

Movado is a high-end watch brand, built with a unique design and a unique slogan, *The museum watch.*

(Movado was the first watch selected for the permanent collection of the Museum of Modern Art.)

After a number of years, the Movado Group decided to "generalize" the watch's slogan to *The art of time.*

The museum watch.

The art of time.

Modern ahead of its time.

Apparently, Movado had second thoughts about *The art of time* and currently uses the marketing slogan *Modern ahead of its time* in an effort to connect the "ahead of its time" idea to the Museum of Modern Art.

Museum is a specific, tangible, memorable word.

Modern is an abstract word that could be associated with any brand, product, service or institution, including a museum.

Keep in mind that words alone will never have the emotional impact of words combined with visuals. It's the difference between the word *sex* and a visual of the sexual act.

(That's why my Visual Hammer book should be read in combination with my Battlecry book.)

The word *museum* suggests a building housing historical artifacts. That made *The museum watch* memorable, especially when Movado's advertising mentioned its selection by the Museum of Modern Art.

The Movado Group itself demonstrates the power of specific words over abstract words. For 35 years, it was known as the North American Watch Co. Then in 1996, in effort to increase the company's visibility among Wall Street analysts, it changed its name to Movado.

It was not an easy decision. The company also markets watches under the Piaget, Corum, Concord and ESQ brands.

In spite of that fact, North American Watch Co. decided to use its core brand and most-popular line as the new name of the company.

And the company is doing well. In 1996, the year North American Watch changed its name to Movado, the company had revenues of $186 million and a net profit margin of 5.2 percent. In 2014, Movado had revenues of $587 million and a net profit margin of 8.8 percent.

As is often the case, you need to sacrifice something in order to find specific words to use in both brand names and slogans.

Sara Lee followed the same path taken by Movado. For 46 years, the company was known as Consolidated Foods Corp.

Then in 1985, it changed its name to Sara Lee. But lately, Sara Lee has gone backwards. In 2012, the company split into two groups.

Hillshire Brands Company, headquartered in America and

Old name.   **New names.**

D.E. Master Blenders 1753, headquartered in the Netherlands.

Neither name has the simplicity and memorability of Sara Lee. *Master Blenders* are two words easily confused with other companies.

Hillshire has a different problem. A mind works like Google does. It thinks ahead in order to anticipate what a person is likely to say.

When a mind hears the first syllable *Hill* and then the "s" sound of the second syllable, it jumps to the conclusion that *Hillside* is the name. That's likely to keep *Hillshire* from becoming well-known.

Like Sara Lee, Kraft Foods has also split up. One company consisting of the North American grocery business is called *Kraft Foods Group.*

The other company consisting of the global snack-food businesses is called *Mondelez International.*

(*Mondelez* is a mash-up of the Latin words for *world* and *delicious.* The name was coined by two employees after Kraft held a contest that drew about 1,700 entries.)

Like Hillshire, the *Mondelez* name is unlikely to become famous. Too many people are going to say, *Monde What?*

Monde, however, is a good choice. *World* in French is *monde.* In Italian: *mondo.* And in Spanish: *mundo.*

It's the *lez* that makes the name useless.

Almost every word near and dear to management people are useless in constructing a slogan that sticks in the mind.

Words like: *Quality, excellence, durable, perfect, exceptional, prime, superior, long-lasting, low-maintenance, choice, deluxe, outstanding, superb, superlative, unrivaled, unparalleled, unsurpassed.*

Abstract words like these need to be brought down to earth before they can be used in creating a memorable slogan.

Take the automobile industry. There are 23 brands that each sell more than 100,000 vehicles a year.

Do you remember any of the 23 slogans used by these 23 brands? I mentioned four of them (all using abstract words) in Chapter 1. By now, you probably have forgotten them.

There is, however, one automobile slogan you might remember. That's the slogan for BMW. Let's see how the slogan was developed.

What do consumers look for when they buy a car?

Everything. They walk around the vehicle to check how its looks. They make sure the interior is nice. They note the expected gas mileage. They put the kids in the back seat to see if there's enough room.

They read Consumer Reports to check on its reliability. They glance at the sticker to check the price.

Then they ask to take it for a test drive.

That's why many automobile manufacturers run advertising that tell the whole story about their "all-new" model-of-the-year vehicles.

When BMW arrived in America some 50 years ago, the car company followed a similar path.

Early BMW advertisements claimed just about everything.

Here are typical headlines from old BMW ads.

A decade later, in 1974, BMW sold just 15,007 vehicles in the American market.

Which made the BMW brand

Our new BMW is a unique combination of luxury, performance and handling. And it's amazingly easy on fuel.

For performance, handling and great fuel mileage, my new BMW has got to be the best engineered car in the world.

the 11th largest-selling European imported vehicle in the U.S. market.

In other words, BMW was going nowhere.

The following year, BMW's new agency (Ammirati Puris AvRutick) launched an advertising campaign that would make both the brand and the agency world-famous.

The ultimate driving machine.

In the decades that followed, BMW became the largest-selling luxury-vehicle brand in the world.

The ultimate driving machine may be the most effective battlecry ever created. It took an also-ran and made it into a leading brand.

So what is BMW doing lately? Don't ask.

Instead of *driving*, BMW has shifted gears and now promotes *Joy.*

JOY WAS BORN FOR THE LEFT LANE.

34

Launched in 2010, the *Joy* campaign had an immediate effect. BMW has fallen behind its archrival Mercedes-Benz.

After having outsold Mercedes in America for nine straight years, BMW now has trailed Mercedes for five years in a row,

Why in the world did BMW take a different road in its marketing? Because it wanted to "broaden" its approach.

Here is what one consultant hired to measure campaign results said: "*Joy* is intended to appeal to consumers who are not necessarily driving enthusiasts, but love to live life."

"The *Joy* campaign represents a stark departure from *The ultimate driving machine* brand message in an effort to reach new audiences and position BMW for broader appeal."

Invariably, when you broaden your appeal, you use abstract words like *joy* or *performance* instead of a specific word like *driving*.

Driving evokes a visual image of two hands on a steering wheel maneuvering a car around winding roads. What image does *joy* evoke?

Every effective marketing program is a compromise.

You need a broad-enough target audience to justify the program in the first place. But you also need a narrow-enough target audience in order to use specific words.

Listen to the way consumers talk. It's only politicians and ad people who speak in generalities. Consumers prefer the specific.

Why do consumers call a table designed to hold many beverages a *coffee table?*

Coffee table.

Wouldn't it be more logical to call it a *beverage table?*

Why do consumers call a case designed to hold clothing, shoes, toiletries and other personal items a *suitcase?* Wouldn't it be more logical to call it a *clothing case?*

Or why is a case designed to hold documents called a *brief case* instead of a *document case?*

Only lawyers call their documents "briefs."

Why do consumers call a store that sells toiletries, cosmetics, snacks, beverages, school supplies, greeting cards and drugs a *drugstore?*

Wouldn't it be more logical to call it a *personal-items store?*

Drugstore.

Or perhaps a *pharmacy,* a name displayed prominently on every "drug" store?

A *gas station* often includes a convenience store, a car wash and automobile-repair facilities.

Yet consumers still call it a *gas station.*

Consumers know a *coffee shop* sells more than coffee. A *steakhouse* sells more than steak. A *grocery store* sells more than groceries.

Specific names that conjure up mental images are more powerful than abstract names.

In the academic world, what do researchers call a 50-page document they might have spent months or years working on? *A paper.*

What does a professor call a position at a prestigious university named after a famous person? *A chair.*

What does a business executive call an appointment to serve on the board of directors of a Fortune 500 company? *A seat.*

Burger King is a better name for a food chain than *Sandwich King. Red Lobster* is a better name for a seafood chain than *Red Seafood.*

Boston Chicken is a better name than *Boston Market.* Chicken is a lot more specific than Market.

Which is the better name?

Then why did *Boston Chicken* change its name to *Boston Market?*

Good question. Especially since shortly after the name change, Boston Market, Inc. went bankrupt.

Specific names are much more effective than abstract names. They also make more memorable slogans.

A fun car to drive.   *Innovation that excites.*

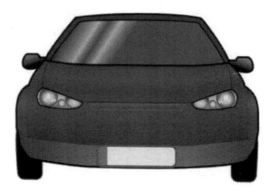

Chapter 3

SELLING VS. TALKING

Some slogans are *selling* slogans and some are *talking* slogans. Let's explore the difference.

Let's say you went to your local supermarket today, a weekly chore. When you got home, you spread your purchases on the kitchen table. Heinz ketchup, Campbell's chicken-noodle soup, Ken's ranch dressing, Barilla pasta and perhaps a dozen other items.

My question is, How many of these brands were first-time purchases? Brands you never bought before.

My guess is that few were first-time buys. Consumers tend to buy what they have bought before. It takes something unusual to get a consumer to switch brands.

But isn't that what brand owners are trying to do with the massive amounts of advertising spent each year? ($160 billion in a recent year.)

Get consumers to switch from competitive brands to their own brands?

Consumers are saturated with advertising everywhere.

The average consumer

in America is exposed to $515 worth of advertising every year.

But surprisingly, when consumers try a new brand for the first time, they are more likely to have been influenced by friends and relatives than they were by the brand's advertising.

That's the power of "word-of-mouth."

Advertisers know this, of course, but they can't do much about it, except to continue to try to reach consumers who might be influenced by advertising. I disagree. They can do something about it.

Consider some internet brands that grew rapidly with no ads at all.

How come these brands were so successful that they were sold for billions of dollars?

Instagram Sold to Facebook for $1 billion.

tumblr. Sold to Yahoo for $1.1 billion.

Zappos Sold to Amazon for $1.2 billion.

Since word-of-mouth is even more important than advertising, it can be particularly effective to make your marketing slogans *word-of-mouth friendly.*

In other words, make them *talking* slogans, not *selling* slogans.

Put yourself in the place of a consumer who already uses your brand. Then ask yourself, Can that consumer use your slogan to recommend your brand to other people?

Suppose you are a BMW owner and someone asks you, How do you like your car? Your first response is likely to be, *It's a fun car to drive.* After all, BMW is *The ultimate driving machine.*

Most automobile brands fail this word-of-mouth test.

Consider the advertising slogans of Hyundai, Nissan and Jeep, three brands that each sell more vehicles a year than BMW.

"Why did you buy a Hyundai?" *I wanted new thinking.*

HYUNDAI *New thinking. New possibilities.*

NISSAN *Innovation that excites.*

Jeep *The best of what we're made of.*

"Why did you buy a Nissan? *I wanted exciting innovation.*

"Why did you buy a Jeep? *I wanted the best of what Jeep is made of.*

How can a consumer "verbalize" any of these automobile slogans without sounding stupid?

These three slogans might have meaning for potential customers, but once customers buy the cars, the three slogans contain absolutely no *talking* points.

Next to a home, an automobile is likely the most-expensive purchase a consumer will ever make. People like to "brag" about their vehicles. Auto companies should help customers by using slogans that provide language they can use to brag about their purchases.

In today's over-communicated society, it's more important to design slogans for word-of-mouth than it is for word-of-selling.

There's another advantage of *talking* slogans over *selling* slogans. Researchers from the University of Warwick in the United Kingdom and University of California, San Diego, tested volunteers to determine how well they remembered text from Facebook as compared to books.

The Facebook posts were remembered one-and-a-half times better than sentences from books. Apparently, our brains favor spontaneous writing (think talking points) over more-polished content.

As a talking point, perhaps the best marketing slogan ever written was the McDonald's slogan: *You deserve a break today.*

It's easy to visualize someone saying to you, *Let's go to McDonald's. You deserve a break today.*

That's music in the ears of mothers everywhere.

On the other hand, some ideas are more powerful *selling* tools than *talking* tools. Hyundai has made great progress in the American market by marketing inexpensive vehicles. But that's not a good *talking* tool.

"Why did you buy a Hyundai?" *Because it was cheap.*

That's not an answer most consumers would use.

Most companies know this. Low price is not a good strategy unless it can be combined with a positive attribute that gives the buyer of the inexpensive product a good *talking* tool.

In our work with Chinese automobile company Great Wall Motor, we suggested they position their low-end Haval brand with the slogan, *The leader in economical SUVs under 100,000 RMB.*

(In American money in the year 2009, about $14,000.)

In other words, position Haval as the leader combined with low cost.

"Why did you buy a Haval SUV?"

It must be a good SUV because it's the leading brand.

Leader in economical SUVs under 100,000 RMB.

Political campaigns are a good example of the power of *talking* versus *selling* slogans.

Voters talk about the candidates they prefer even more than consumers talk about the products they prefer.

Smart politicians provide their supporters with *words* they can use in speaking up for their candidacies.

Take the recent Presidential elections. Barack Obama's campaigns were clearly superior to those of his opponents.

In his 2008 campaign, his slogan was *Change we can believe in.* It's easy to visualize an Obama supporter saying, *After eight years of George Bush, we need a change.*

What was John McCain's slogan? He ended up with *Country first.* But earlier in his campaign, it was *Best prepared to lead from day one,* as well as *Reform. Prosperity. Peace.*

None of these three slogans made good talking points.

"Why are you going to vote for John McCain?"

Because I put my country first.

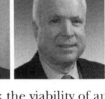

Change.   **Country first.**

Not a likely response from a voter. One way to check the viability of any slogan is to reverse the slogan and pin it on your opponent.

If McCain is *Country first,* then Barack Obama is *Country second.*

That doesn't ring true to any fair-minded individual.

In 2012, Barack Obama's slogan was *Forward.* The implication, of course, was to continue on the course he had set in his first term.

Forward.   **Believe in America.**

Mitt Romney's slogan was *Believe in America.*

"Why are you going to vote for Mitt Romney?"

Because he believes in America. Not a likely response.

Again, let's reverse the slogan and see if it rings true. *Barack Obama doesn't believe in America.*

That's highly unlikely. Barack Obama doesn't believe in the country that made him rich and famous as well as a recipient of a Nobel prize?

Visa had a long-running ad campaign that was particularly effective in driving consumer word-of-mouth. *It's everywhere you want to be.* In another words, it's accepted in more places than any other card.

Sorry, we don't take American Express. Many consumers have gotten turndowns like this in shopping trips here and abroad.

After 24 years, the slogan was changed to *Life takes Visa.*

Why the change? I can only guess it was advertising-driven.

Life takes Visa makes a better-looking advertising campaign.

Recently, wiser heads at Visa have apparently realized the error of their ways and the company is back to the original slogan with a twist: *More people go with Visa.*

That's not, however, a better word-of-mouth slogan that the original. Consumers don't want to think they just "go along with the crowd." Consumers wants to think they are special.

So Visa went back to its original slogan, but with one word deleted. *Everywhere you want to be.*

Hey Visa, here is a slogan that puts the idea into words a consumer can instantly understand: *Accepted in more places than any other card.*

This slogan can be used as a *talking* point by many Visa customers. Why do you carry a Visa card?

Because it's accepted everywhere.

Chapter 4

TAGLINES VS. SLOGANS

When Tom Bodett was recording a radio commercial for Motel 6 back in 1986, he found the script was a few seconds short.

So to finish the spot, he ad-libbed a few words.

The line was an instant hit with consumers everywhere. Even today,  almost 30 years later, Tom Bodett's Motel 6 spots end with the tagline, *And we'll leave the light on for you.*

That's what most taglines do, including *Leaving the light on,* a spontaneous and loving thing people say to each other. But it does not position the Motel 6 brand, nor is it very truthful.

"We don't actually leave the light on for you," confided Tom Bodett. "We just say that to be friendly. You have to turn it on yourself once you enter the room."

Taglines can be cute, funny, flippant or irrelevant, but they generally have little to do with what makes a brand successful.

They're like road sweepers and clean-up crews at the end of parades. They call attention to the fact that the commercial has come to an end. But they seldom have anything to do with positioning the brand.

Radio and television newscasters used to end their nightly broadcasts with taglines, some of which became very famous.

Good night and good luck, the tagline of Edward R. Murrow.

And that's the way it is, the tagline of Walter Cronkite.

Both men went on to become two of the most-respected newscasters in the broadcasting industry.

While a number of taglines like *And we'll leave the light on for you* can be exceptionally memorable, they seldom help position the brands. They are throwaway lines that could apply to any brand.

Any hotel can leave the light on for you. And any newscaster can wish you good night and good luck.

Even nonsensical taglines can be memorable. Old-time comedian Jimmy Durante used to end his television broadcasts with the tagline: *Good night, Mrs. Calabash, wherever you are!*

No one has ever found out who Mrs. Calabash was and what her relationship to Jimmy Durante might have been. (Probably a joke.)

What's missing in most taglines is motivation. They don't provide a reason for buying the brands.

Slogans are different. A good slogan sums up a company's strategy. Why stay at Motel 6? Not because they leave the light on for you.

Check Motel 6's website and you'll find the answer to that question: *Lowest price of any national chain.*

That's the real slogan for Motel 6, an idea they should hammer in everything they do. (But in a more memorable way.)

Even Edward R. Murrow, who became famous in World War II with his nightly broadcasts from London during the Battle of Britain, had a slogan that pre-dated *Good night and good luck.*

He started every broadcast with three words. *This . . is London.*

Like all effective slogans, this one captured the essence of what his broadcasts were all about: London's ordeal during the Blitz.

In spite of the sorry history of taglines, the advertising industry has been quick to drop slogans and jump on taglines.

Why would an industry noted for creativity be so willing to embrace the tagline concept? Especially since the word connotes a secondary, throwaway idea. ("The last line of an actor's speech" is the dictionary definition of tagline.)

Take Shakespeare's most-famous monologue, *To be or not to be? That is the question.*

Do you happen to remember the tagline for Hamlet's soliloquy? Most people don't. Here it is: *Be all my sins remember'd.*

In the context of Hamlet's speech, that's an emotional ending, summing up the reasons for the difficulty he had making decisions. But it's not the theme of the soliloquy.

To be or not to be? That's the theme, or slogan if you will, a theme that still resonates today, more than 400 years after Shakespeare wrote it. It's one of the most-memorable lines in English literature.

Many marketing people, including possibly readers of Battlecry, consider "taglines" and "slogans" to be two names for the same thing. But they're not.

A tagline is the last line of a speech. It's the way marketing people often end their advertisements and commercials, integrating a tagline with the brand's logotype.

Here are some four current examples from the automobile industry. All these taglines are short.

The four taglines average just 2.5 words each.

There's a strong preference for short taglines, presumably because it's easier to integrate

a logotype with just a few words. But that can undermine your ability to use the memory-enhancing techniques outlined in this book.

Our experience shows that marketing slogans need not be short. Some of the most memorable slogans have been quite long.

When it absolutely, positively has to be there overnight. Nine words that made FedEx Corp. one of the largest air-cargo carriers in the world. An example how "repetition" can create a memorable slogan.

The word "slogan" is an ancient word with a long history starting with the Celtic tribes of Ireland, one of the great civilizations of Europe, with artisans, literature and a system of laws.

By the ninth century, many Celts from northeast Ireland began moving to the western islands of Scotland where they were known as "Scottish Gaels" and their language as "Scottish Gaelic."

"Sluagh gairm" is a Scottish Gaelic word for "gathering cry" and in times of war for "battle cry." (Sluagh, meaning people or army and gairm, meaning call.) Sluagh gairm made its way into English as slughorn, sluggorne, and eventually slogan.

Over the years many slogans were used as battlecries, an example being *Dieu et mon droit* (God and my right) of the English kings.

During the Battle of Crécy in 1346, this was Edward III's battlecry.

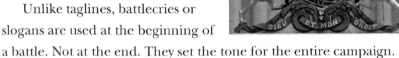

What part *Dieu et mon droit* played in Edward III's victory is unknown, but obviously the English longbow played a major role.

Unlike taglines, battlecries or slogans are used at the beginning of a battle. Not at the end. They set the tone for the entire campaign.

Our Revolutionary War in the 1770s used a number of battlecries. *Liberty or death. Join or die. Don't tread on me!*

Finally, *Don't tread on me!* became the most-used battlecry of the American Revolution with the rattlesnake as the visual symbol. (An example of how a verbal nail works well with a visual hammer.)

A generation later, the dispute with Britain over the northern border of the Oregon territory produced another memorable battlecry.

The British wanted the border between what is now Canada and the United States to be set at the 42nd parallel, while the Americans wanted it set at the 54th parallel and 40 degrees.

Tempers raged on both sides with Americans in Oregon territory loudly proclaiming *Fifty-four forty or fight!*

Two wars with Great Britain were apparently enough (1776 & 1812), so President James Polk settled on the 49th parallel.

Later in the 19th century, a rebellion in Cuba over Spanish rule put an autonomous government in place.

But 11 days after the new government took over, Spanish officers ignited a riot in Havana. To protect the safety of its American citizens, President William McKinley sent the battleship USS Maine to Havana.

Three weeks later, a massive explosion occurred and the USS Maine sank in the harbor killing 266 American sailors.

It's never been quite clear what caused the explosion, although the U.S. Navy at the time concluded that the ship's magazines were ignited by an external explosion under the ship's hull. Nevertheless, newspapers in the United States responded with bitter denunciations of the Spanish.

**Remember the Maine.
To hell with Spain!**

The public took up the battle with the cry: *Remember the Maine. To hell with Spain!*

After the turn of the century, America was involved in World War I, one of the most brutal wars in history with 15 million deaths.

Over time, the war became known as *The war to end all wars.*

What makes a military battlecry memorable?

Don't tread on me!

Fifty-four forty or fight!

**Remember the Maine.
To hell with Spain!**

The war to end all wars.

It's instructive to look at these four American battlecries and see what makes them memorable.

Of the four military slogans, the least striking is *Don't tread on me!* The other three are exceptionally memorable.

Unless you are a historian, you are unlikely to remember the slogan *Don't tread on me!*, even though it was part of the most-important war America has ever fought.

(The Tea Party uses a *Don't tread on me* flag as its unofficial symbol, but I doubt future generations will remember the slogan.)

The mental glues that make the other three slogans memorable are: Alliteration, rhyme and repetition.

Alliteration: *Fifty-four forty or fight!*

Rhyme: *Remember the Maine. To hell with Spain!*

Repetition: *The war to end all wars.*

Then there's the soul-stirring battlecry of the French Revolution, the national motto of France.

Most Americans know the national motto of France, but how many Americans know the national motto of the United States?

Liberté • Égalité • Fraternité

RÉPUBLIQUE FRANÇAISE

In God we trust is the official national motto of the United States, as established in a law signed by President Eisenhower in 1956.

It replaced the unofficial motto *E pluribus unum* used since 1782 when it was incorporated in the "Great Seal of the United States."

In God we trust appeared on coins in 1864 and on paper currency in 1957. It was first used as a battlecry during the American Civil War by the 125th Pennsylvania Infantry at the Battle of Antietam

Most Americans are aware of *In God we trust* and *E pluribus unum*, but they don't stir the emotions like *Liberté. Égalité. Fraternité.*

That's the inherent problem with too many mottos and slogans. They are created by people who focus on the "content" of the message rather than on the "memorability" of the slogan.

Without memorability, a slogan is unlikely to accomplish much.

In the chapters that follow, I will discuss in detail five techniques to create memorable slogans: Rhyme, alliteration, repetition, reversal and double-entendre.

But these need not be used in isolation. You can combine them in order to create slogans that will last for generations.

Consider this proverb created by Benjamin Franklin. In 14 words, Franklin used four memory techniques a total of six times.

One repetition: *Early & early.*

One reversal: *To bed & To rise.*

Two alliterations: *Makes & man.* *Wealthy & wise.*

Early to bed and early to rise, makes a man healthy, wealthy and wise.

And two rhymes: *Rise & wise.* *Healthy & wealthy.*

No wonder *Early to bed and early to rise* has lasted for 280 years.

Birds of a feather . .

. . flock together.

Chapter 5

RHYME

In legal circles, Gerry Spence was known as the "best trial lawyer in America." In 41 years, he has never lost a criminal jury trail.

According to one source, "He no sooner makes the decision to take on a client, then he drafts his closing statement coming up with a catch phrase he repeats throughout the trial."

"Let us select a phrase, a theme, a slogan," wrote Gerry Spence, "that represents the principal point of our argument."

"The theme can summarize a story that stands for the ultimate point we want to make."

In the Karen Silkwood case, he told the jury the story of a citizen who brought a lion onto his property that somehow escaped and mauled his neighbor.

Then he related that story to a case against the Kerr-McGee Corp. which had stored an inherently dangerous substance on its premises.

He then combined the two with the slogan: *If the lion gets away, Kerr-McGee must pay.*

And Kerr-McGee did pay. $10,500,000 to Karen Silkwood's children.

That's the same strategy used by lawyer Johnnie Cochran in the 1995 murder trial of O.J. Simpson.

In the trial, O.J. had difficulty trying on a leather glove used in the murders of his ex-wife Nicole Simpson and her friend Ronald Goldman.

Said Johnnie Cochran: *If the glove doesn't fit, you must acquit.* And the jury did acquit O. J. Simpson.

Every year, Lexus runs one of the most-memorable ad campaigns, *December to Remember.*

December to remember.

For 18 years in a row, Lexus has run TV commercials featuring vehicles adorned with big red bows.

The television pitch is basically a special deal on Lexus vehicles during the holiday season.

The American automotive industry spends about $16 billion a year on advertising, most of it on television commercials.

The Lexus brand accounts for less than 2 percent of this total and its *December to Remember* television commercials account for just a fraction of that 2 percent.

Yet many consumers remember the *December to Remember* spots. Much of the other 98 percent is totally forgotten.

Simple ideas set in rhymes can be highly effective. One example is the U.S. Postal Service, one of the biggest businesses in America with 488,000 employees and annual revenues of $68 billion.

If it fits, it ships.

To promote its many services, the Postal Service spends many millions of dollar on advertising.

Do you remember any of its past advertising campaigns? You probably only remember *If it fits, it ships.*

A good slogan doesn't necessarily have to tell the whole story, especially when the whole story is complicated.

If it fits, it ships sums up the idea that the U.S. Postal Service has different-size boxes, each of which can be shipped for one flat rate.

So if you can manage to stuff everything into one of their boxes, it can be shipped at an attractive price.

The Postal Service could have said, *Now, four flat-rate boxes that can be shipped anywhere in the country for one flat rate.*

That's the message all right, but a message expressed in a way few people will remember.

What about smaller companies? Can they use rhymes to establish their brands? Of course they can. You don't need a big budget and a television campaign to establish a memorable rhyme.

A seafood restaurant in Brockton, Massachusetts, has become locally famous with a clever rhyme.

The fish you buy today swam last night in Buzzard's Bay.

McMenamy's Seafood could have just said, *We sell fresh fish,* which is the essence of its message. But the rhyme takes the *fresh fish* idea and makes it memorable.

Where I live, the largest provider of services to homeless people is Atlanta Union Mission. But its slogan, *Saving lives with your help,* didn't communicate very much.

Ending homelessness.

Recently, the nonprofit decided to adopt a new name and a more memorable slogan. *Atlanta Mission: Ending homelessness.*

(The rhyme inside the word *homelessness* makes the "homeless" concept more memorable.)

ATLANTA MISSION

One of the best examples of a national brand created by a rhyme is Pepsi-Cola. Back in the 1930s, when the country was in a depression, the Pepsi-Cola company started running radio commercials comparing 12-oz. bottles of Pepsi with 6.5-oz. bottles of Coca-Cola.

Anyone who grew up in the 1930s and is still alive today most likely remembers those lines.

(My dad does.)

Pepsi was lucky. Today, Coke would have taken them to court over the third line in the jingle:

Twice as much for a nickel too.

Pepsi-Cola hits the spot.
Twelve full ounces, that's a lot.
Twice as much for a nickel too.
Pepsi-Cola is the drink for you.

The more accurate comparison doesn't have the same poetic sound:

Almost twice as much for a nickel too.

Consumers have benefited from rhymes almost as much brands. Rhymes are a convenient way to remember facts helpful in daily life. How much does water weigh?

A pint's a pound the world around.

That makes it easy to calculate the weight of water and most liquids. A quart weighs two pounds. A gallon weighs four pounds.

These are only estimates, of course. A pint of water weighs a little over one pound. Actually: 1 pound, 0.69 oz.

And who could remember the number of days in each month of the year without the rhyme?

Thirty days hath September,

April, June and November.

What is astounding is the long life enjoyed by rhymes and devices that enhance memories.

The thirty-days couplet dates back to the 16th century.

People have learned to be better spellers by repeating the rhyme *I before E except after C.* (I keep reminding people of this rhyme when they ask how to spell Ries.)

Why are rhymes memorable? Even silly rhymes like the ones shown here. To understand why you remember these silly rhymes, consider how the mind works.

That's the story, Morning Glory.
Up your nose with a rubber hose.
A blast from the past.
Liar. Liar. Pants on fire.
No pain, no gain.
Paralysis by analysis.
Shop 'til you drop.
When in doubt, throw it out.

Your mind doesn't file words or phrases or sentences or ideas.

Your mind files sounds. Similar sounds are filed as if they were the same. Words like *principal* and *principle*, for example.

The physical apparatus that organizes the sounds in your mind are the roughly 100 billion neurons in the average brain.

It is the connections between the neurons that account for the power of rhymes and other memory techniques.

With 100 trillion possible connections, it is likely that sounds that rhyme are physically connected in the brain, like the wiring in an electrical device.

That's the story, Morning Glory.
Up your nose with a rubber hose.
A blast from the past.
Liar. Liar. Pants on fire.
No pain, no gain.
Paralysis by analysis.
Shop 'til you drop.
When in doubt, throw it out.

When you hear a saying like *Up your nose with a rubber . . .* , the mind immediately adds the word *hose* to complete the saying.

When you hear a saying like *When in doubt, throw it . .* , the mind immediately adds the word *out.*

When nonsensical sayings like these are locked together in a mind, they are almost impossible to forget.

Then, too, the less sense a nonsensical saying makes, the more likely you are to remember it. That's because a nonsensical saying is different and therefore "shocking."

Take the movie, *Cloudy with a Chance of Meatballs,* a big success earning $243 million. Then there's *Big Ass Fans,* a company growing at the rate of 25 to 30 percent a year. (Previous name: HVLS Fan Co.)

In other words, verbal "shocks" operate much like visual "shocks."

Which of these two faces capture the most attention?

The face that is different and therefore "shocking."

(Evolution produced in our ancestors a visual system sensitive

to change, a useful trait when looking for game or avoiding an enemy.)

When you combine rhymes with "shocking" or unusual words you can create memorable stories, books and television shows.

The 47 children's books written by Dr. Seuss illustrate this principle. The existence of silly rhymes, especially in books written for children, seems to have convinced buttoned-down management types that corporate or brand slogans should avoid rhymes and other memory-enhancing devices. And that brand slogans should be serious.

And not only serious. They should be short, uplifting and focused on the biggest, most-conceptual idea a company can dream up.

Here are the six slogans used in America by the six largest Japanese consumer-electronics companies.

Can you match the slogan to the company? Unless you work for one of the Big Six, you probably cannot.

(The slogans are in the same order as the company logotypes

Inspire the next.	HITACHI
Ideas for life.	Panasonic
Empowered by innovation.	NEC
Leading innovation.	TOSHIBA
The possibilities are infinite.	FUJITSU
Make. Believe.	SONY

on the right half of the illustration.) If a company cannot create a memorable slogan, it's difficult to build a brand. And if a company cannot build a strong brand, it's difficult to make money.

In the past ten years, these six Japanese companies had revenues of $4.1 trillion. (That's trillion, not billion.) Yet these six companies managed to lose $13.1 billion. Even Sony, one of the world's best-known brands, lost $3.6 billion in the past ten years.

One of the problems with these six brand slogans is the fact that they are short. One is four-words long. Three are three-words long. And two are two-words long.

A two-word slogan that rhymes is going to be difficult to create. Even four words are limiting. Yet inside companies, there is pressure to come up with short slogans, partly the result of tagline thinking.

That's only part of the problem. When you make everything under one brand name, as these six companies do, there's nothing specific you can say in your marketing slogan. It has to be a mushy generality.

Take United Airlines long-term slogan. Why in the world would United drop an alliterative slogan that also rhymes in favor of the unemotional *It's time to fly?*

Fly the friendly skies of United.

(It's what a pilot might say to passengers after a long delay.)

Also, the original slogan, *Fly the friendly skies of United,* contains a positive attribute (friendly) that could differentiate the airlines from its competitors.

Tagline thinking seems to be the reason for making the change. (Recently, United has seen the error of its ways and has gone back to its original slogan, *Fly the friendly skies.*)

Take *Ace is the place with the helpful hardware man.* (Nine words.) The long-time slogan for Ace Hardware.

Because of the gender problem and also to shorten the Ace slogan, it was changed to *The helpful place.* (Three words.)

You know what? *The helpful place* might be shorter and it might communicate the same benefit as the original, but it loses the rhyme and memorability of *Ace is the place.*

I would have added two words to the original. A man could speak the words *Ace is the place with the helpful hardware man.*

Then a woman steps out in front of the man and adds the words *And woman.* (For a short time, Ace Hardware did use this approach.)

Take *The best part of waking up is Folgers in your cup.* (11 words.) Two decades ago, Folgers led Maxwell House in coffee by 30 percent. Currently, Folgers' lead is 70 percent.

For a number of reasons, the Folgers slogan is truly remarkable. Coffee is consumed all day long. (Check out Starbucks at 5:00pm.) So why focus on breakfast?

One reason is that it facilitates the rhyme *waking up* with *cup.* The other reason is psychological. If Folgers is good at breakfast, thinks the consumer, it must be good all day long.

Just creating a memorable slogan is not enough. To be effective, the slogan needs to be associated with the brand.

That's why a slogan that also incorporates the name of the brand (*Folgers in your cup*) greatly improves its effectiveness.

Maxwell House's long-time advertising slogan, *Good to the last drop*, while clever is not nearly as effective. Not many coffee drinkers associate *Good to the last drop* with the Maxwell House brand.

While it's very difficult to come up with a short slogan that rhymes, it's not impossible. Take Charles Shaw wine.

The wine was introduced exclusively at Trader Joe's grocery stores in the state of California.

The price? $1.99 a bottle.

Someone had the idea of putting a poster on the top of the Charles Shaw display with a slogan that rhymed.

Two-buck Chuck became America's largest-selling brand of wine in spite of the fact that it was sold in only one retail chain in one state. With no advertising.

Generally, however, slogans need to be relatively long to be effective. Take Alka-Seltzer's slogan: *Plop, plop, fizz, fizz, oh what a relief it is!*

And how about *You scream, I scream, we all scream for ice cream?* Nonsensical, but memorable because of the repetition and the rhyme. *I scream for ice cream* is not nearly as memorable.

Then there's Bounty, *the quicker picker upper.* For some 30 years, Nancy Walker played Rosie, the waitress in a diner who uses Bounty to pick up spills.

This visual consistency plus the memorable verbal rhyme made Bounty the No.1 brand of

paper towel. Today, Bounty outsells the No.2 brand (Kleenex Viva) more than four to one.

In spite of Bounty's long-term success, Procter & Gamble couldn't resist tinkering with the slogan, now in its fourth iteration.

1967 to 1980: *The quicker picker upper.*

1980 to 1994: *The quicker thicker picker upper.*

1994 to 2009: *The quilted quicker picker upper.*

2009 to present: *The thick quicker picker upper.*

Have any of these changes improved the original slogan? Nope. For most people, Bounty is still *The quicker picker upper.*

Another long-running Procter & Gamble advertising campaign featured Mr. Whipple, a fictional supermarket manager who scolds customers for squeezing Charmin toilet tissue.

The joke involves Whipple doing the same thing when he thinks no one will notice. The visual action of squeezing the Charmin helps the brand pre-empt the *softness* attribute.

This simple idea made Charmin the market leader for decades. (Much like *driving* did for BMW. And *breakfast* for Folgers.)

The verbal punch line could have been *Don't squeeze the Charmin* which captures the essence of the *softness* idea. But adding one word greatly improved the slogan.

Please don't squeeze the Charmin is memorable because of the rhyme between *please* and *squeeze.* (Similar to *Ace is the place.*)

Mr. Whipple, played by actor Dick Wilson, was eventually replaced by the Charmin bears, a cartoon family whose parents extol the virtues of Charmin to their cubs.

While the bears are charming in their own way, the *softness* idea that made Charmin the No.1 toilet-tissue brand is totally lost. It's typical of what happens as a brand grows up.

Inside a company, there's enormous pressure to expand the brand, to make it cover more market segments.

So now there are four types of Charmin.

Ultra soft, ultra strong, basic (a euphemism for cheap) and sensitive (a touch of aloe and vitamin E.)

When Charmin was focused on *soft,* Procter & Gamble was able to create a memorable idea, *Please don't squeeze the Charmin.*

Now that Charmin is focused on "soft, strong, cheap and sensitive," it's extremely difficult to come up with a verbal slogan that makes any sense. Hence the bears.

Introduced in 1950, Timex is a watch brand that initially tried to cover many different features.

Print advertisements promoted three features of the Timex brand: Waterproof, dustproof and shock-resistant.

Headline: *Imagine! The features of a $50 watch for only $9.95.*

By 1955, the Timex brand had 15 percent of the total watch market, but then sales stalled.

The following year, United States Time Corp., the owner of Timex, launched a television campaign that would make advertising history.

Using a variety of devices like jackhammers, dishwashers, water-skiers and a dive off the cliffs at Acapulco, Timex watches were put through many torture tests to demonstrate the validity of the slogan.

It takes a licking and keeps on ticking.

Sales boomed. By the year 1970, Timex watches were being sold in 30 different countries. The brand had half the watch market in America and one-third the watch market in England.

Many people still remember, *It takes a licking and keeps on ticking.* Like a diamond, a clever rhyme will last forever.

The lead detective in a recent episode of the TV show *Blue Bloods* was asked how he felt after taking a blow to his "noggin."

It took a licking, he said, *but it keeps on ticking.*

Here are some rhymes most people will remember for decades.

All the news that's fit to print.

Click it or ticket.

Drive sober or get pulled over.

What happens when things change? The New York Times is also on the web, so it changed its slogan to *All the news that's fit to go.*

Before changing a marketing slogan that is universally recognized, the Times should have asked itself, Is this change absolutely necessary?

Most people know that magazines and newspapers are now available in digital as well as printed form.

If the Times prints *All the news that's fit to print,* it will also print *All the news that's fit to go on the web.*

And if FedEx is the best service to use *When it absolutely, positively has to be there overnight,* then it is also a good air-cargo service to use for two and three-day deliveries.

FedEx is a corporation with 162,000 employees and $45.6 billion in annual revenues.

FedEx has been spending more than $100 million a year advertising its services.

FedEx Relax, it's FedEx.

FedEx We understand.

Do you remember any of these recent FedEx advertising

FedEx Solutions that matter.

campaigns? Probably not. Compare Roto-Rooter's slogan ($370 million in annual revenues) with FedEx.

In 1933, Milton & Samuel Blanc fashioned a sewer-cleaning machine from a washing-machine motor, roller-skate wheels and steel cable.

Called Roto-Rooter, the cable rotated sharp blades to cut roots out of sewer lines, eliminating the need to dig up the lines.

The company's service trucks carried a slogan that bragged about

Roto-Rooter, that's the name.

ROTO-ROOTER

And away go troubles down the drain.

Roto-Rooter's patented technology. But it wasn't until 21 years later that the company adopted the slogan that would make its brand famous.

Inside corporations today there is enormous pressure for employees to innovate. The future belongs to companies that can create innovative new products and services.

Back in the year 1933, Roto-Rooter was an innovative new product. But what maintained the brand's leadership for eight straight decades was the simple rhyme: *Name* and *drain.*

As proof, ask yourself, What's the No.2 brand of sewer cleaner?

One measure of success is the absence of strong competitive brands in the category.

Heinz in ketchup. Hellmann's in mayonnaise. Kleenex in tissue. Roto-Rooter in sewer cleaners.

Many other rhymes have influenced consumers for a very long time. Take the apple, for example.

Have you ever noticed how many magazines use apples as symbols for articles on health and wellness?

And many health groups use an apple as a visual symbol.

How did apple-mania affect so many organizations?

Check history. In the 1920s,

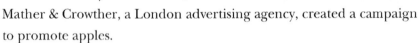

Mather & Crowther, a London advertising agency, created a campaign to promote apples.

Its slogan: *An apple a day keeps the doctor away.*

That's all it took to lock the apple with the concept of healthy eating. When a publication runs a "health" article they frequently use an apple.

And look at the number of logotypes that use an apple to symbolize food in general.

Instead of an apple, why not an orange, a peach, a banana, a pear, a grape, or a lime?

If I were to pick the healthiest fruit, I would choose a blackberry.

Of course, these things can work in reverse. Look at what a jingle has done to the perception of baked beans.

Beans, beans, the musical fruit.

The more you eat, the more you toot.

Too bad. Because of their high-fiber content, beans are a nutritious and healthy food. (The tooting is sound evidence of that.)

Now if we could figure out a good word that rhymes with "fiber," maybe we could fashion a memorable jingle that would do for beans what Mather & Crowther did for apples.

One useful trick in developing a brand's slogan is to ask yourself, What's already in consumers' minds?

Take wine, for example. In 2010, at an auction in Hong Kong, a bottle of Châteaux Lafite-Rothschild 1869 was sold for $232,692.

What does that tell you? Old wine is much better than new wine, an insight that led to the slogan, *We will sell no wine before its time,* for the Paul Masson brand.

People are brands, too. If you can rhyme an attribute to a person, you can often create a slogan that will last for decades. For example, *Stan the Man Musial,* the baseball player.

No drama, Obama.

Elvis, the pelvis.

Also, *No drama, Obama.*

And, *Elvis, the pelvis.*

Many brands are hydra-headed. They vacillate between two slogans.

The state of Florida, calls itself *The Sunshine state* on license plates, but also spends a lot of money promoting Florida as *The vacation state.*

I would have tried to combine the two ideas in a single slogan.

Florida: No.1 to the sun.

Leadership is always a good component of a marketing slogan.

If a brand is the leader in its

No. 1 to the sun.

FLORIDA

category, thinks the typical consumer, it must be better than the others.

Chapter 6

ALLITERATION

With a name like Smucker's, it's got to be good. That's the way
I keyboarded the slogan in the first draft of this book.

Whoops! After a quick Google search, I found the slogan really is:
With a name like Smucker's, it has to be good.

Think of the way a mind works. Starting with the key word *good,*
a mind quickly jumps to the alliterative word *got,* rather than *has.*

In truth, the Smucker's slogan is memorable enough as it is.
But most slogans could be improved with a dose of alliteration.

The thought comes first. Then a mind searches its memory for words
to express the thought. And once a mind latches onto the first word,
its natural tendency is to reach out to other words that are alliterative.
Just as I reached out to the word *got* after starting with the word *good.*

This experience demonstrates one of the most important principles
of human memory systems.

The neurons in your brain have obviously many more connections
to alliterative "sounds" than they do to sounds that are not alliterative.

The more alliterative words you use, the more likely your slogan
will be remembered. Like Brycream's slogan: *A little dab'll do ya.*

Even better are alliterative slogans that include the brand name:
Fixodent and forget it.

Even though your advertising slogan is unquestionably memorable, consumers will still have to connect your slogan with your brand name, or you will have wasted your money.

Alliteration is the glue that make slogans stick in consumers' minds. When trying to come up with a name, consumers will search their minds for alliterative words to connect with fragments of what they remember.

While rhyming is an exceptionally-powerful memory device, there are actually more opportunities to use alliteration than rhymes.

Take product names. I could only think of five names that rhyme: *Steak & Shake, Shake Shack, Walkie Talkie, Hobby Lobby* and *Fitbit*.

But quite a few brand names are alliterative. Here are six of them.

With 26 letters of the alphabet and a speaking vocabulary of some 5,000 words, the average word has almost 200 alliterative possibilities.

In the past, some alliterative ideas that were almost nonsensical

became famous. It was Spiro Agnew, Richard Nixon's Vice President, who referred to the liberal media as *nattering nabobs of negativity*.

Even though you had to use a dictionary to decode what he meant, the *nattering nabobs* quote resonated with the media and the public.

The more alliterative words you string together in a brand's slogan, the more memorable it becomes. For example: *Debbie Does Dallas.*

Here are nine more alliterative slogans and sayings.

One very effective technique is to combine an alliterative brand

Cash for clunkers.
Feed a fever, starve a cold.
He who laughs last, laughs best.
March Madness.
The terrible twos.
The fickle finger of fate.
Toys for tots.
Waste not, want not.

like M&Ms with a slogan that is also alliterative: *Melts in your mouth. Not in your hands.*

Alliteration of *M* and *Ms* with *melts* and *mouth* almost guarantees the brand would become a big success.

Companies that are planning to launch new brands often contact us. "After our naming firm develops a brand name," prospects often tells us, "we want to set up a strategy session with you."

"Do the opposite," we usually tell the prospects. "Do the strategy first and then select a brand name that connects with the strategy."

Using, of course, one or more of the verbal techniques in this book as well as one of the visual techniques outlined in Visual Hammer.

Of the two, strategy and brand name, the strategy is more important. But if consumers cannot connect your strategy with your brand name, then you aren't going to be successful.

One of the best examples of the power of alliterative brand names like *M&Ms, Honey Baked Ham, Tater Tots* and many others is the story of the *Range Rover* brand.

The company that manufactures the Range Rover is Land Rover, a firm that has made four-wheel drive vehicles in the United Kingdom for many decades. (Now called Jaguar Land Rover, the company is owned by Tata Motors of India.)

Land Rover makes Land Rover and Range Rover models, but the Range Rover brand is much better known among car buyers.

Since Range Rover is well-known and Land Rover is not, many people think Range Rover is the company name and Land Rover is a model.

That's the power of an alliterative name like *Range Rover.*

One of the most difficult categories to launch a successful new brand is charities and foundations. More than a million such organizations are registered with the Internal Revenue Service.

If you are Bill Gates with a net worth of something like $80 billion to fund your organization, you don't need a create a memorable name. The Bill & Melinda Gates Foundation, or B&MGF, will do quite nicely.

That's not the position John Melia was in. While serving in Somalia, he was severely wounded in a helicopter crash.

A decade later, with the help of family and friends, Melia founded the *Wounded Warrior Project.*

Prior to a 2005 incorporation, the *Wounded Warrior Project* operated as a subsidiary of the United Spinal Association of New York. During this period,

the organization developed its trademark activities, delivering backpacks full of supplies and other items to the bedsides of injured soldiers.

In the past decade, the *Wounded Warrior Project* has grown rapidly, thanks in part to its striking trademark and its alliterative name.

In 2013, the charity raised $224 million.

Alliteration can be a powerful force in the brand-building process, but it can also be a hazard.

In the 1980s, Chevrolet was marketing eight different car models, only two of which were not alliterative with Chevrolet. (Ones in blue.)

The other six models were alliterative with Chevrolet.

In one sense, that makes sense. Consumers would see a Chevette on the road and connect it with the core brand, Chevrolet. That's good.

Chevrolet models in the 1980s.

Chevette	Camaro
Citation	Corvette
Cavalier	Celebrity
Malibu	Monte Carlo

In another sense, it's not. Consumers would see Chevrolet models, all starting with the letter "C," and wouldn't be able to differentiate one model from another. That's bad.

Today, Chevrolet markets nine different car models, but only four of which use alliterative names, so they're making progress.

The function of model names is to allow consumers to distinguish one model from another. For example, a Chevrolet Corvette from a Chevrolet Malibu, and then file them in separate locations in the mind.

But alliterative model names do the opposite. They lock models together in the mind, confusing consumers.

Often, that's exactly what a company wants to do. Lock the words in a slogan together. Or lock the slogan to the company's brand name.

But sometimes you don't. Why would the United States government lock *Medicaid & Medicare?*

Two different programs for two different groups.

When you hear the words *Social Security,* you quickly know what the program is and for whom it was designed. But when you hear the word *Medicaid* or the word *Medicare,* you have to think about it a while to figure out what the name refers to.

And unless you are a participant in either *Medicaid or Medicare,* you probably don't know one program from the other.

Take the *IRS* and the *FBI.* Everyone knows the two agencies as: (1) *Internal Revenue Service* and (2) *Federal Bureau of Investigation.*

Now suppose you wanted to apply Medicare/Medicaid thinking to the two names. You might keep *Federal Bureau of Investigation,* but change the *Internal Revenue Service* name.

The *IRS* is not really *Internal* since they collect from all citizens wherever they live. And *Service* is a generic word that could be used by any government agency. That leaves the key word *Revenue.*

So suppose you do the following.

FBI . . . Federal Bureau of Investigation.

FBR . . . Federal Bureau of Revenue.

The *FBI* and the *FBR* would cause endless confusion. Don't laugh. In corporations, this type of thinking occurs often.

Some parents consider themselves clever when they give children alliterative names like: Ralph, Robert, Roger and Ryan.

Thereby causing lasting problems for friends and relatives who will never be able to tell them apart.

On the other hand, many parents overlook the advantage of giving a child a first name alliterative with the child's last name.

71

How does one get famous? You have to do something, of course, to deserve the fame only the media can provide. But it's helpful, too, if your name is memorable like these alliterative names.

Ronald Reagan   Mickey Mantle   Mickey Mouse

Marilyn Monroe   Roy Rogers   Robert Redford

Yet, the statistics show parents actually avoid using alliterative baby names.

For surnames, the five leading letters of the alphabet are: M, S, W, B and H, accounting for 43 percent of all surnames in America.

Yet in a recent year, these five letters account for none of the five leading baby names.

For baby names, the five leading letters are: A, C, J, E and L. Together these five letters account for 34 percent of baby names.

Take the letter "A" which accounts for 14 percent of baby names, yet only 3.4 percent of surnames.

When choosing a brand name, there's another aspect of alliteration companies need to be aware of.

There is a strong correlation between brand and category names. Quite often the leading brand in a category is alliterative with the name of the category.

Here are some examples.

(More brands would use category alliteration if more marketers were aware of the power of this phenomenon.)

Beer — Budweiser
Cola — Coca-Cola
Crayons — Crayola
Cruises — Carnival
Gin — Gordon's
Beans — Bush's

There's a mental reason why the names of many leading brands are alliterative with their category names. Nobody just buys a brand.

Nobody walks into a retail store and says, *I'd like to buy a Sony. Would you show me all the Sonies you have to sell?*

Consumers think first about category and second about brand. Then they might go to Best Buy and look at Sony TV sets.

Category first, brand second. That's the way consumers decide what to buy and then what brand to buy.

Now look at how new categories develop. A new category often starts with literally hundreds of brands.

In personal computers, for example, there were hundreds of brands, including big-name brands like those shown here.

When a prospect thinks of buying a personal computer, it would be difficult to find a connection in the prospect's mind between the concept of a *computer* and many of these companies.

Imagine trying to find a connection between *computer* and AT&T, a brand strongly identified with *telephones.*

And Dictaphone, *a voice recorder.*

And Exxon, *a gasoline station.*

And Motorola, *a car radio.*

And Xerox, *a copy machine.*

Most of the other personal-computer brands had similar problems. Even Apple, a pioneer in personal computers, was associated with *home* personal computers and not *office* personal computers.

That's one reason Apple never became the leader in office personal computers after the introduction of the IBM 5150, the first serious 16-bit office personal computer.

Nor did IBM's leadership last very long. What was IBM's problem? In spite of the fact the company was first in office personal computers, the brand itself was identified with *mainframe* computers.

As happens in many categories, the long-term leader turns out to be the only brand not associated with anything except the category itself. In other words, a new brand with no baggage from the past.

In the computer category, the Compaq brand had a big advantage. Because of alliteration, many people could have jumped from the idea of buying a *computer* to buying a *Compaq computer.*

Compaq was not only alliterative with *computer,* but it was also the only computer brand name that included an attribute.

Not surprisingly, Compaq was the No.1 global computer brand for five years in a row before its 2001 acquisition by Hewlett-Packard.

H-P then made a serious error by putting its resources behind its *Hewlett-Packard* brand, in essence killing its *Compaq* brand.

In a new category, alliteration is an especially important concept. It's smart to pick a brand name alliterative with the category name. *Silk soy milk. Magic markers. TurboTax tax-return software.*

So what happened when Silk introduced a new category called almond milk? They forgot about alliteration and used the Silk name.

(A better name for the brand might have been *Amen almond milk. Amen* is double alliterative with *almond.*)

Look at maid service, a developing category which could explode as the economy improves. Three brands use memory-enhancing names.

Two alliterations, *Molly Maid* and *Merry Maids,* and one rhyme, *Maid Brigade.* That's unusual.

Most new categories have almost no brands that utilize these powerful techniques.

The motion-picture industry should be big users of alliteration and other memory-enhancing techniques.

Not so. I did a survey of 100 classic motion pictures and found only four with alliterative titles: *King Kong, Marathon Man, Dirty Dancing* and *The Naughty Nineties.*

(*King Kong* is an example of how long a really great name can last. It was first exhibited 82 years ago)

Only five of the 51 films that Woody Allen has directed have alliterative titles: *Manhattan Murder Mystery, Bullets Over Broadway, Whatever Works, Magic in the Moonlight and Don't Drink the Water.*

You might think many television shows would be using alliteration. Most don't, but some do.

Candid Camera, Duck Dynasty, Keeping up with the Kardashians, Mad Men and *Breaking Bad* are shows that owe some of their success to their alliterative titles.

And look at an annual summer concert series held at Lincoln Center in New York City and built around the music of Mozart.

They could have been called *The Mozart Festival,* but they weren't. They were called *Mostly Mozart* and are still going strong after 49 years.

Then there's *Meatless Monday* dreamed up in 2003 by Sid Lerner, an advertising agency executive.

After discovering he needed to seriously lower his cholesterol level, he asked nutrition experts how much saturated fat should be removed from his diet to make a meaningful difference in health.

The answer? Fifteen percent, just one day's intake.

Celebrities like Paul McCartney, Oprah Winfrey, Richard Branson and Yoko Ono have expressed their commitment to *Meatless Monday.*

Peggy Neu, director of the *Meatless Monday* program said recently: "Our research shows that nearly one in five Americans participate and avoid meat on Monday at least occasionally." Why Monday?

"People view Monday as a day for a fresh start and a chance to set healthy intentions," explained Neu. (Ironically, no mention by Neu that *Meatless Monday* is also alliterative.)

We live in Atlanta where the transportation system is called "Marta." (Metropolitan Atlanta Rapid Transit Authority.)

Like in most cities, commuters in Atlanta prefer to drive their cars rather than use public transportation. Many Atlantans have never used Marta. To encourage people to try the system, we suggested they introduce *Marta Mondays,* a day everyone rides free.

Marta Mondays.

You might think that this would drastically reduce transit revenues, but that's not so. Most passengers buy weekly or monthly tickets.

What it might do is to stimulate trial, the first step in convincing commuters to switch from roads to rail.

Political slogans tend to be ultra-short. *Forward* for Barack Obama and *Believe in America* for Mitt Romney in 2012.

Yet one of the most effective political slogans was 15 words long.

It helped a relatively-unknown congressman become the mayor of New York City.

After eight years of charisma and four years of the clubhouse, why not try competence?

Ed Koch composed a slogan that characterized two previous New York City mayors.

The *eight years of charisma* referred to former mayor John Lindsay and the *four years of the clubhouse* to former mayor Abraham Beame.

In the opinion of voters, both John Lindsay and Abraham Beame deserved the putdowns.

Charisma, clubhouse, competence are a classic "one, two plus three" approach. If the typical voter knows the first two statements are correct, then the third statement, by inference, must also be correct.

That's not the only memorable slogan created by Mayor Ed Koch who greeted New Yorkers with the slogan, *How'm I doin'?*

One of the truisms of politics is that no elected official leaves office with his or her reputation intact.

Therefore a good strategy is to run against the previous office holder as Ed Koch did. Not against your opponent.

Even a trivial concept can get famous by putting alliteration to work. Back in 1991, a hamburger chain, Rally's, ran a TV commercial starring 17-year-old Seth Green.

Every time an item was added to a customer's order at a place called Pricey's, Seth Green would echo the cash register with a loud *Cha-Ching* and a karate move.

The point of the TV commercial was that "add-ons" at other chains rapidly ran up the price, while a meal at Rally's was only $1.97.

Cha-Ching lives on today as an expression for something expensive. It's also the name of a personal-finance app as well as the title of a book by Time Reid on small-business marketing.

One of the largest annual meetings is the Comic Book Convention held in San Diego. Every year, more than 130,000 fans show up.

In 1995, the convention's name was officially changed to *Comic-Con*, driven by fans who began using a short-hand version of the name, Comic Book Convention.

The new Comic-Con name helped to generate a lot of PR and there's a reason why.

Three generic words strung together (comic & book & convention) don't sound important. Any group could hold a comic book convention. A grade school, a high school, a Boy Scout troop.

Comic-Con is a brand name that can register in consumers' minds as something special. Then, too, the name is alliterative with a second quality called "inverse" alliteration.

The "C" of *Con* repeats the sound of both the first and last letters of the word *Comic*. Therefore, the name *Comic-Con* benefits from both alliteration and inverse alliteration.

Peo-ple is an alliterative word.

Ap-ple is an inverse-alliterative word.

There are not many inverse-alliterative brand names. In a survey of several hundred brand names, we found only eight.

Words with repeating consonants usually are inverse alliterative. *Mis-sis-sip-pi* is a highly-memorable word. It contains one alliteration and three inverse alliterations.

Inverse alliteration doesn't always need repeating consonants.

Canon, the Japanese camera company, is an inverse-alliterative name because it is pronounced *Can-non*.

Compound words that are alliterative also make good brand names. A good example is *BlackBerry*.

A useful trick is to capitalize both words as *BlackBerry* does rather than use the name as a dictionary suggests.

Butterball turkeys, for example, uses a trademark with its name in all-capital letters, *BUTTERBALL*, which is never a good idea.

Capital letters are harder to read than upper-and-lower-case letters. But there's another reason for upper-and-lower-case letters.

ButterBall is how we would have set the type for the turkey brand. The dual caps emphasize the alliteration.

As a memory device, alliteration is both easy to do and very effective. Who can forget the line, *Peter Piper picked a peck of pickled peppers?*

Much more memorable than: *Peter Smith gathered a lot of peppers he hoped to sell.*

Furthermore, the original has two examples of "double alliteration." *Peter* with *peck* and *peppers*. And *Piper* with *picked* and *pickled*.

(The second word in a double alliteration (*Peter* and *peck* repeat the first two letters of the first word.)

And consider the "hate" group, the *Klu Klux Klan*. But that's not its real name. It's *Ku Klux Klan*.

But the double alliteration of *Klux* and *Klan* is so powerful that most people assume the full name must be *Klu Klux Klan*.

Ku Klux Klan.

Alliteration is the one of the most-effective tools in your marketing tool kit and it's one of the easiest to use. Just get yourself a spelling dictionary and look up all the words that are alliterative with your brand name.

You might find another *Melts in your mouth, not in your hands.*

How much wood would
a woodchuck chuck

if a woodchuck
could chuck wood?

Chapter 7

REPETITION

Alliteration is difficult. Rhyme is even more difficult. Yet repetition is easy. Just repeat some of the thoughts in your slogan.

Then why do so few companies use repetition?

I think I know the answer to that question. With the average slogan just four words long, there's obviously a strong trend toward brevity.

Also, what used to be *slogans* are now called *taglines.*

When it absolutely, positively has to be there overnight.

A long tagline? That doesn't make sense.

Yet, long slogans can make a lot of sense. Take Federal Express. The air-cargo company didn't say: *When it has to be there overnight.* Instead, its nine-word slogan turned FedEx into a global cargo giant.

Even now, you'll find the words *absolutely, positively* used in stories about FedEx even though it's been decades since the air-cargo carrier had used the slogan.

Absolutely, positively a force in China

FedEx CEO saw market potential 20 years ago

This newspaper clipping is from USA Today. *Absolutely, positively a force in China* says the headline.

81

Take another look at Shakespeare's famous line, *To be or not to be?* He could have said *To be or not?* which has exactly the same meaning. But what's missing is the poetry and symmetry of the original.

You might say the addition of the second *to be* did for Hamlet what *absolutely, positively* did for Federal Express.

Consider the last four slogans of the U.S. Army.

Which one of the four slogans do you remember?

My guess it's the second one, *Be all you can be*, a slogan the

Today's Army wants to join you.
Be all you can be.
An Army of one.
Army strong.

Army has not used for more than a decade. Like the Shakespeare quote, the slogan was longer than needed. It could have read: *Be all you can.* The extra *be* doesn't add anything except poetry and symmetry.

The other military services have also had problems developing long-term memorable slogans. After many tries, the U.S. Air Force developed what is known as a "call and response."

The call is *Aim high* followed with the response: *Fly-fight-win.*

Aim high is certainly in the right direction for the U.S. Air Force because it's a double-entendre. But it needs something to complete the thought. What do you get by aiming high?

The response, however, is terrible. *Fly-fight-win.*

Granted, *Fly* and *flight* are alliterative, but saying those two words rapidly together is almost impossible. It's a tongue-twister.

A better direction might have been *Aim high and win.*

The United States Navy doesn't have an official motto or slogan, but *Non sibi sed patriae* is often considered its unofficial slogan. (*Not for self but for country.*)

The winner among military slogans is the Marine Corps with six words everybody remembers.

The few. The proud. The Marines.

The Marine slogan is a good example of the importance of sentence structure in communicating an emotional message. It's one thing to say: *Marines are few and proud.*

It's another thing to say: *The few. The proud. The Marines.*

The repetition of a relatively-unimportant word like *The* elevates the slogan to a much-higher emotional level. The slogan also dramatizes the exclusivity of being a member of the Marine Corps.

The few. The proud. The Marines, the slogan that built a brand and a dedicated organization.

Toms Shoes is a for-profit company that also operates a nonprofit subsidiary, Friends of Toms. Founded in 2006 by Blake Mycoskie, the company designs and sells shoes as well as eyewear.

For every pair of shoes that Toms sells, another pair of shoes is given to an impoverished child.

Toms Shoes' slogan is simple and unforgettable: *Buy one. Give one.*

Repetitive words seems to strengthen almost every marketing slogan. Some examples.

Don't clean it, OxiClean it.

Life is our life's work. (Pfizer.)

The milk lover's milk. (Mayfield.)

Better ingredients. Better pizza. Papa John's.

What happens here, stays here. (Las Vegas.)

An effective slogan often generates parodies. A T-shirt my sons wear: *What happens at Grandma's, stays at Grandma's.*

Slogans, of course, are not the only factor that determines who wins and who loses in a marketing battle. Obviously products play a role.

Every marketing situation is a combination of products, features, prices, distribution and slogans. You can't win with a bad product and a good slogan.

But you can lose with a good product and a bad slogan.

Take the non-caloric sweetener market. One of the first products was cyclamate which was banned in 1970 after lab tests in rats indicated that large amounts of cyclamates caused bladder cancer.

That left saccharin as the only alternative, a product still used in brands like Sweet'N Low.

The next product breakthrough was aspartame sold as Equal and NutraSweet. Aspartame quickly become a big seller because it eliminated some of the bitter aftertaste of saccharin.

What slogans were used by Equal and NutraSweet? I don't know. Maybe the owners of these brands figured they didn't need them because the product itself was such an improvement over saccharin.

That often happens. And it is true that a breakthrough brand doesn't need a slogan. The product speaks for itself.

That's true today. But what about tomorrow?

Enter Splenda, the first brand of sucralose. What product advantage did Splenda bring to the market? I don't know and as far as I can tell, sucralose does not have much of an advantages over aspartame. If any.

But it did have a powerful slogan that made Splenda the leader in non-caloric sweeteners: *Made from sugar so it tastes like sugar.*

At one point, the Splenda brand had a 49 percent market share versus a 17 percent share for Equal.

Next up is stevia, the first "natural" non-caloric sweetener to make a name for itself in America.

Truvia (Coca-Cola & Cargill) and PureVia (PepsiCo & Merisant) are two stevia brands.

Truvia's marketing slogan: *Nature's calorie-free sweetener.*

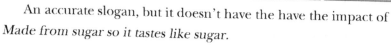

An accurate slogan, but it doesn't have the have the impact of *Made from sugar so it tastes like sugar.*

The category demonstrates the challenges innovations create for existing brands. If it weren't for the Splenda brand, Equal would be a successful brand today.

(In 2009, Merisant, the owner of Equal, declared bankruptcy.)

So every leader brand needs to prepare for the introduction of a revolutionary new brand that will disrupt the category.

There are no guarantees, but a slogan can provide some protection from future competition.

Take the pain-reliever category. The long-time category leader was Bayer aspirin first introduced in 1899 (with Aspirin as its brand name.)

After the loss of its Aspirin trademark, the American owners of the brand switched to "Bayer" as the brand name.

Acetaminophen was first launched as a prescription drug with the brand name Tylenol and later went over-the-counter.

But it wasn't until 1975 that Tylenol began to run advertising that would make the brand famous. Headline of the first advertisement: *For the millions who should not take aspirin.*

The copy went on to say: "Aspirin can irritate the stomach lining . . . cause small amount of hidden gastro-intestinal bleeding."

The headline was the slogan. It even appeared on the package. (Always a good idea, but seldom done.)

Then Sterling Drug, the owner of the Bayer brand, made a mistake. *No, Tylenol is <u>not</u> found safer than aspirin* was the headline of the first Bayer advertisement to attack its rival.

Then they seemingly backtracked on that idea by introducing Bayer acetaminophen, the non-aspirin pain reliever.

What should Bayer have done? Exactly what they are doing now with the slogan: *The wonder drug that works wonders.*

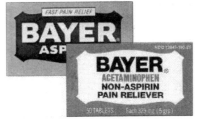

The packages, however, just say *The wonder drug.* The short slogan just doesn't have the same effect as the long slogan. There is something powerful about repetition that defies analysis.

Next up was Advil in 1984. Initially the brand did exceptionally well by positioning its two competitors as "out of date."

An aspirin tablet was marked "1899." A Tylenol tablet "1955." And an Advil tablet "1984."

Hence the 1984 Advil slogan: *Advanced medicine for pain.*

A great idea in the short term, but not necessarily in the long term, thanks to Aleve introduced in 1994. 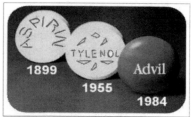 (In 2005, Bayer bought Aleve from Roche Consumer Health.)

Aleve based its positioning strategy around the long-lasting idea. As the packages say, *All-day strong. Strength to last up to 12 hours.*

But the advertising has not been very consistent. Typical headline: *If you would take fewer pills, why wouldn't you?*

Aleve has a significant product difference, but needs to hammer that difference with a simple, memorable slogan.

Look what a simple, memorable slogan did for Walmart.

Again, the repetition of *always* created a slogan that I'm sure was recognized by the vast majority of the American public.

Walmart also used the slogan on the exterior of its stores.

But how about Walmart's latest slogan? *Save money. Live better.*

Like the original slogan, the new Walmart slogan is only four words, but there's no repetition. There's no alliteration. There's no rhyme. In fact, it's two separate ideas: *Saving money* and *living better.*

Sure, the two have an intellectual connection, but who is going to take the extra time to make the connection?

Two ideas are not better than one. Actually, they are a lot worse.

Since Walmart switched slogans, the chain has been losing ground to its rivals. Whether the new slogan is the cause is hard to tell.

Walmart's long-term success is based on a retail concept called "everyday low prices." But most chains have a different strategy.

Most retail chains practice what the trade calls "high/low pricing." In other words, a regular schedule of sales. In the last few days I noticed advertisements from the following chains.

Bloomingdale's . . . 50% to 75% off.

Lord & Taylor . . . . Up to 80% off

Macy's . . . . 25% to 60% off.

Back in 1979, Little Caesars pioneered a totally different approach. "Every day a sale day." The slogan: Two great pizzas for one low price.

Pizza is ideal for a price-cutting approach, with the lowest ingredient cost of any restaurant entree. Approximately 25 percent. Other dishes, like seafood, can range up to 50 percent.

By 1988, Little Caesars was the third-largest pizza chain in America after Pizza Hut and Domino's.

Pizza Hut . . . . . $3,240 million.

Domino's . . . . . $2,500 million.

Little Caesars . . $1,130 million.

In 1989, the following year, Little Caesars launched a TV campaign that boiled the slogan down into two unforgettable words which they also used on exteriors.

Pizza! Pizza!

It is amazing what a simple repetition can achieve.

In 1994, a USA Today panel of top ad-agency creative directors named Little Caesars as "the best advertising campaign of the year."

Thanks in part to its brilliant marketing program, that was the year Little Caesars became the second-largest pizza chain in America.

Pizza Hut . . . . . . $5,400 million.

Little Caesars . . . $2,050 million.

Domino's . . . . . . $1,973 million.

The following year, the tinkering began, starting with a major tinker. The company converted 30 takeout units in the Detroit, Michigan area to "Little Caesars Italian Kitchens."

Besides pizza, the new menu included lasagna, chicken, salads, dessert pies and pasta. (Tortellini, penne and farfalle.)

By 1995, Little Caesars expected to operate 100 Italian Kitchens. Needless to say, that never happened.

In 1996, Little Caesars rolled out *Delivery. Delivery.* The takeout-only chain was now going to compete head-to-head with Domino's, the home-delivery leader.

That same year, Little Caesars also launched *Pizza by the Foot.* Nearly four feet of food.

Little Caesars rolls out delivery delivery

A "safety video" was a creative twist to the chain's *Pizza by the Foot.* Customers had to watch the safety video before leaving the restaurant. Of course, few customers ever watched it.

In 1997, the chain introduced *Big! Big! Pizzas.* How big were they? As Little Caesars' advertising said, *Bigger than the sun!*

Little Caesars' large pizza was 65 percent bigger than Pizza Hut's and Domino's. Little Caesars' medium pizza was 77 percent bigger. Little Caesars' small pizza was the same size as their large pizzas.

A good idea, but somewhere along the way the *Pizza! Pizza!* concept disappeared in a cloud of creative confusion.

In the midst of all these changes, you seldom heard a word of caution from industry pundits. Quite the opposite.

"Industry analysts say that by adding home delivery," according to USA Today, "Little Caesars can boost its business without purchasing a lot of costly equipment."

Said another expert said, "You're at a competitive disadvantage if you're in the pizza business and not delivering."

That's common sense which is just not the same as marketing sense. Common sense says a second slogan is additive. "Little Caesars is known for takeout, so we'll launch delivery. That way we'll own two ideas."

Marketing sense is subtractive. A second slogan seldom gets accepted because the new slogan conflicts with the old one in consumers' minds.

Even worse, a second slogan often undermines the existing one.

So where is Little Caesars today? Back in third place. Here are 2014 system-wide sales for the three chains.

Pizza Hut . . . . . . $5,500 million.

Domino's . . . . . . $4,116 million.

Little Caesars . . . $3,405 million.

What is Little Caesars current slogan? Who knows? Many consumers still have that *Pizza! Pizza!* refrain bouncing around in their heads.

Short slogans might be good for inexpensive products like pizza, but not necessarily for expensive products like car insurance.

Take Geico, for example. In 1996, when the company was acquired by Warren Buffett's Berkshire Hathaway, Geico had less than 3 percent of the automobile insurance business.

Today, it has more than 9 percent and the brand is neck-and-neck with Allstate, the No.2 car-insurance company.

What tripled Geico share of the car-insurance market? One factor is an advertising slogan that has run continuously for 16 years.

Here's what Warren Buffett had to say about Geico in 2012: "Berkshire's insurance operations shot the lights out last year. It generated $73 billion of free money for the company to invest."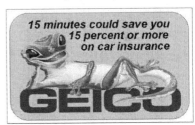

"This is having your cake and eating it too," said Warren Buffett. "When I count my blessing, I count Geico twice."

In an era where "50 percent off" the retail price is a typical discount, what made Geico's "15 percent off" so effective?

Two things. (1) The consistency of Geico's 15-percent message which has been running for 16 years.

And (2) The memorability of the 15 percent message achieved by connecting the percentage with the notion of "15 minutes."

The truth is, the longer you keep repeating an advertising message the more believable it becomes.

State Farm, the market leader, is using a similar repetition strategy involving the word "state." *State Farm: Get to a better state.*

What's wrong with State Farm's slogan? *State* is an abstract word, almost useless in a marketing program.

The only specific word in the company's name is the word *Farm,* but they wouldn't use it in a slogan because it limits the market.

Simple, specific ideas expressed in a repetitive way can have enormous consequences.

Lee Iacocca was a 22-year-old engineer who had just completed Ford's training course. He told his superiors he wanted a job in sales rather than engineering.

When nobody at Ford headquarters would give him a sales job he quit and went to Pennsylvania and got a job in a Ford regional office. In 1956, Lee Iacocca devised a plan that would make him famous.

His *'56 Ford for $56 a month* caught the eye of Robert McNamara, a group executive, who took the plan nationwide and brought Iacocca back to headquarters.

Just four years later, he became Ford division general manager.

In Iacocca's long career, he was president of Ford Motor Company and chairman of Chrysler Corp.

He also appeared on the cover of Time magazine three times.

One of his first tasks at Chrysler was to introduce the company's "K" car. Once again, Iacocca made advertising history with his slogan: *If you can find a better car, buy it.*

Another example of repetition is an Ad Council's campaign in cooperation with the U.S. Dept. of Health to reduce drunk driving.

The ad campaign could have said: *Don't let friends drive drunk.* But they added a word. *Friends don't let friends drive drunk.*

When you compare the two, you'll notice a shift in emphasis from "keeping" a friend from driving drunk to "proving you are a friend" by keeping that friend from driving drunk.

Not only does it increase the motivation of consumers to take action, but also it increases the memorability of the slogan. Surveys show that 90 percent of adults are aware of the slogan.

And the results of the ad campaign are also positive. In a decade, the percentage of traffic fatalities due to alcohol-related accidents decreased from 60 to 45 percent.

Another good example of repetition is the Old Spice campaign featuring Isaiah Mustafa. *The man your man could smell like.*

And the alternative form: *Smell like a man, man.*

The Isaiah Mustafa campaign reversed years of decline of the Old Spice brand.

Recently, Old Spice has been increasing its market share in both deodorants and body wash.

Chapter 8

REVERSAL

Time wounds all heels is a memorable saying because it's a reversal of the old epigram: *Time heals all wounds.*

Interestingly enough, the old epigram is also an example of reversal. The words *heals* and *wounds* are the opposite of each other.

The punchline of a joke is often a reversal. The setup from a 1930 Groucho Marx movie: *One morning I shot an elephant in my pajamas.* The punchline: *How he got into my pajamas, I don't know.*

Then there is the famous conversation between Amos and Kingfish on the old Amos 'n' Andy radio show.

Amos: *Where does good judgment come from?*

Kingfish: *Well, good judgment comes from experience.*

Amos: *Then, where does experience come from?*

Kingfish: *From bad judgment.*

Many well-known brands have been built using a similar technique. After the failure of the Webvan Group, the company that pioneered Internet grocery deliveries, another company jumped into the market. (In two years of operation, Webvan lost $830 million.)

Instead of trying to build a national company like Webvan Group, Fresh Direct focused its activities on the metropolitan New York market. (Focus is a particularly important concept for a startup.)

93

Fresh Direct also developed a very effective marketing slogan using the concept of reversal.

**Our food is fresh.
Our customers are spoiled.**

Instead of losing millions, Fresh Direct has managed to become profitable in a very difficult business.

Currently, the company has over $100 million in annual sales. Time is also on the company's side.

As the economy improves, home delivery of groceries could experience rapid growth.

In literature and in history, the most-memorable ideas tend to be expressed in polar opposites, or reversals.

And so, my fellow Americans, ask not what your country can do for you, ask what you can do for your country. John F. Kennedy.

It was the best of times, it was the worst of times . . . Charles Dickens.

Some say the world will end in fire, some say in ice. Robert Frost.

The late Charles Revson borrowed the idea from Robert Frost and introduced a cosmetic line called *Fire & Ice.* Which promptly became Revlon's most successful product.

And who can forget the name of the most-famous motorcycle club in the world?

Do you know the name of any other motorcycle club?

Hearing or reading a "reversal" is like watching a tennis match.

Reversals vibrate between

two opposite meanings, forever embedding the concept in your mind.

For example: *No good deed goes unpunished.*

The political truism: *You can't beat somebody with a nobody.*

And Peter Drucker's axiom: *Management is doing things right. Leadership is doing the right things.*

One of the major problems we face in our consulting assignments is that clients often want slogans that are instantly meaningful.

The pursuit of perfection is a nice slogan for Lexus because it leaves nothing to the imagination. But that's not necessarily an advantage. Slogans that are instantly meaningful are often not very involving.

The reader thinks, O.K., I get it. Lexus is perfect. So what?

Often, the most memorable slogans are not complete in themselves. They force the prospect to think, What does that mean?

Take the Holiday Inn slogan which the chain used for many years: *The best surprise is no surprise.*

The reversal in the Holiday Inn slogan is a jolt to the imagination, but it doesn't answer the question, What do they mean by "no surprise?"

Readers of Holiday Inn advertisements quickly found out that every Holiday Inn has air-conditioned rooms, a restaurant, conference rooms, a pool and a cocktail lounge, among other things.

There's no surprise. A night in one Holiday Inn is like a night in any other Holiday Inn.

That's why Holiday Inn's slogan, *The best surprise is no surprise,* is remembered by many prospects while most hotel slogans are not.

Some current examples from Hilton, Ritz-Carlton and Hyatt.

Recently, Holiday Inn launched a new campaign to try to re-capture the magic of its previous slogan. New slogan: *Changing your view.*

The television commercials show guests being treated like family, enjoying their stay whether they are traveling for leisure or business.

Without a memorable slogan, the *treated like family* message is likely to be totally lost.

More than 90 percent of all ad slogans are expressed in the positive, but expressing an idea in the negative is often more powerful.

Google could have used a positive internal slogan like *Do good.* But who would have remember that? Instead the reversal, *Do no evil,* also captured the imagination of many people outside of Google.

At last count, there were more than 1.5 million nonprofit groups in America, most with very limited budgets for communications.

One way for a nonprofit to get into the minds of potential donors is by using a memorability technique like reversal.

Take Autism Speaks, an organization that sponsors autism research and public awareness activities.

Founded just ten years ago, the organization has become the largest nonprofit devoted to autism advocacy and research.

AUTISM SPEAKS

It's time to listen.

The Autism Speaks slogan is a reversal and the name is a double-entendre since many autistic children are not verbal.

The puzzle piece reflects the perspective of a parent or guardian to whom the autistic person is a problem to be solved.

Sara Lee could have said: *Everybody likes Sara Lee.*

But instead they said it in the negative and in a long, rambling way: *Everybody doesn't like something, but nobody doesn't like Sara Lee.*

A long and complicated slogan, but exceptionally memorable.

Back in 2006, Sara Lee dropped the *Nobody doesn't like* slogan in favor of: *The joy of eating.* A positive slogan nobody will remember.

Some powerful slogans don't seem to be reversals until you consider the environment in which they were launched.

For example, the notion of "thinking before you act" is ingrained in consumers' minds.

Yet Nike launched a campaign that implied just the opposite.

Just do it became a rallying cry of the younger generation.

JUST DO IT.

Nike has been using the slogan for 27 years, one of the few slogans that have lasted this long.

Advertising Age selected Nike's *Just do it* as the second-best slogan of the 20th century. Second only to *A diamond is forever.*

Advertising Age also selected the 100 best advertising campaigns of the 20th century. The No.1 campaign was also based on reversal.

Think small was the headline of the first Volkswagen Beetle ad. That was also the theme of the campaign including ads like these.

It makes your house look bigger.

And if you run out of gas, it's easy to push.

Live below your means.

Volkswagen also ran an ad featuring the 7-foot, 1-inch basketball star Wilt Chamberlain trying to get into a Volkswagen.

The domestic auto industry was focused on "big" in 1950, the year the Beetle arrived.

Think small was negative in the sense that consumers preferred larger vehicles.

When you challenge the prevailing opinion, you force consumers to re-think their own positions.

That's why the Volkswagen campaign made such a deep impression on the public, much like the Nike campaign *Just do it.*

When going against public opinion, it's also important to do so in a light-hearted way. If you are too serious, you instantly turn off consumers who may have a different opinion than your own.

Even the consumer who prefers big, luxurious vehicles had to agree there's some merit in the idea, *Live below your means.*

We once suggested to Eatzi's, a gourmet takeout-food chain, that they use an idea that states what Eatzi's stood for.

The idea, of course, is a reversal of *Joy of Cooking*, a famous book that has sold 18 million copies since it was first published in 1931.

For some reason, retail chains seldom display slogans on their stores. Yet they often pay thousands of dollars a month for billboards.

And those billboards are often within walking distance of the stores. That makes no sense.

The best place for an advertising slogan is over the front door of a retail establishment. It provides a reason for a passer-by to walk in.

The advantages of takeout gourmet food like EatZi's are obvious, but sometimes the benefits of a new brand in a new category are not.

Dial was one of the first deodorant soaps and eventually Dial became the long-time category leader.

But an explicit message like *The first deodorant soap* might have generated nothing but yawns and a *Who needs it* response on the part of consumers.

Aren't you glad you used Dial soap? Don't you wish everybody did?

The Dial campaign that did run used "reversal" to get consumers involved in the benefits of the brand. Nobody knows how they smell.

The reversal *Don't you wish everybody did?* creates uncertainty among consumers about how they might smell to others.

That's true, thinks the consumer, I know people with offensive odor. I'd better use Dial to make sure I'm not one of them.

"Involvement" is one of the major keys to the success of your ads. You need to get the consumer involved, not just in the product itself, but also in the advertising. To build a brand, you need to do both.

One brand that did both is Clairol. Years ago, many women felt they could only get their hair colored at a hairdresser.

Hair-coloring kits were messy and didn't work very well.

Clairol's strategy? Challenge the reader to decide.

Does she . . . or doesn't she color her own hair?

The other half of the slogan was the answer to that question.

Does she . . . or doesn't she?

Hair color so natural only her hairdresser knows for sure.

In other words, you can't tell the difference.

Does she or doesn't see? not only made Clairol the leading brand, but it also convinced many women that they didn't need a hairdresser. They could color their own hair.

Another reversal campaign that built a leading consumer brand was an advertising program featuring Frank Perdue and his chicken.

For 23 straight years and some 200 TV commercials Frank Perdue hammered his *Tough man* concept, turning Perdue into the first national brand of chicken.

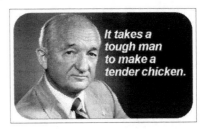

It takes a tough man to make a tender chicken.

At his death in 2005, Perdue Farms was selling $2.8 billion worth of tender chickens every year.

To drill an advertising message into a human mind requires a focus, consistency and especially patience. Take United Negro College Fund (now known as UNCF.)

It was 44 years ago that Young & Rubicom along with the Ad Council created the slogan, *A mind is a terrible thing to waste.*

In those 44 years, The United Negro College Fund has helped more than 300,000 students obtain undergraduate and graduate degrees.

The Association of National Advertisers has 522 member companies that account for a significant share of all advertising run in America.

How many of their advertising slogans have been used for 44 years? Or even 22 years? You could count them on the fingers of one hand.

Another leader brand created by a reversal campaign is Secret, the first antiperspirant/deodorant made for and marketed to women.

Many advertising slogans are developed exactly the wrong way.

The company and its ad agency do research to find out what ideas

Strong enough for a man, but made for a woman.

are circulating in consumers' minds. Then they jump on the idea that seems to touch the majority of their prospects.

What do consumers want from a high-tech company?

Innovative new products. So that would seem to call for a slogan that dramatizes how innovative a company is.

Here are some companies that have used the word *innovation* in their slogans in the past few years.

Agilent Technologies: *Innovating the HP way.*

ASUS: *Inspiring innovation. Persistent perfection.*

Bosch: *We bring innovation.*

Firestone: *A tradition of innovation.*

Ford: *Driving American innovation.*

NEC: *Empowered by innovation.*

Nissan: *Innovation that excites.*

Siemens: *Global network of innovation.*

Toshiba: *Leading innovation.*

Now, do you remember any of these slogans? And has any slogan convinced you to buy one of the company's *innovative* products?

Like many other abstract concepts, *innovation* is a useless word in marketing messages.

Slogans need to be brought down to earth. They need to touch people in surprising ways. And reversals are one way to do that.

Fram became famous as a manufacturer of automobile filters with a series of television commercials starting back in the 1980s.

You can pay me now, or pay me later says an automobile mechanic, explaining to a customer that he can either pay a small sum now for replacing an oil filter or a larger sum later for replacing an engine.

Both the reversal plus the slogan's "incompleteness" explain why it's so memorable. *Pay me later* for what?

The engine. Oh, I get it.

Fram could have said it directly: *If you don't replace your oil filter, your car's engine might need replacement.* That's the same idea said in a straight-forward, dull, uninteresting way.

You can pay me now, or pay me later is a great slogan because it combines reversal with incompleteness and repetition.

Of all the techniques you could use to make a slogan memorable, *reversal* is probably the easiest and the most effective. Some examples.

Broiling, not frying. Burger King.

Imported from Detroit. Chrysler.

It's not a room, it's a residence. Residence Inn.

The uncola. Seven-Up.

Two great tastes that taste great together. Reese's peanut butter cups

The biggest little city in the world. Reno, Nevada.

The quality goes in before the name goes on. Zenith.

Almost any idea can be reversed, although many don't make sense. But sometimes they do.

Who would have thought you could reverse *chicken soup* and wind up with *soul?*

Rejected by 144 publishers. Now has 250 titles. Sold more than 500 million copies.

When a reversal makes sense, it is both memorable and shocking.

When you read or hear something you don't expect to read or hear, you pay attention.

A diamond is forever.

Chapter 9

DOUBLE-ENTENDRE

A *reversal* has two meanings and so does a *double-entendre*.
But the two meanings embedded in a double-entendre are contained
in a single word or phrase.

A diamond is forever also means a love symbolized by a diamond
can last forever, too.

With a large percentage of single women living with their boyfriends
before marriage, the engagement ring has become almost as important
as the marriage license.

Ask a woman how her relationship is going and a typical comment
might be, *Great, but I still don't have a ring.*

(A man who is second-in-line for the British throne can get away with
a sapphire engagement ring, but commoners better not try it.)

Double-entendres can be powerful because the double meanings
can be encased in short, simple, memorable phrases.

How many other inexpensive
food products like Morton salt,
less than a dollar a container,
have advertising slogans that
have lasted for over 100 years?

None, that I know of.

When it rains, it pours.

When it rains, it pours was first used in 1911 to dramatize the fact that the salt was free-flowing in rainy weather because an absorbing agent was added. The first try, *Even in rainy weather, it flows freely,* didn't have the emotional impact of the double-entendre.

Oddly enough, the slogan itself doesn't appear on current packages. But it doesn't matter since the Morton girl, now in her fifth iteration, communicates the message.

Needless to say, Morton is the No.1 brand of salt by a wide margin.

A double-entendre is particularly memorable when the word is easily visualized. Pouring rain and pouring salt, for example.

Merrill Lynch is the best-known stock brokerage firm in America. One reason is its slogan developed in 1973 by Ogilvy & Mather.

The origin of the terms *bull* for a rising market and *bear* for a declining market are unclear, but they date back to the early 20th century.

Merrill Lynch is bullish on America.

It took many decades before Merrill Lynch pre-empted the *bull* idea for its advertising slogan. But why didn't another brokerage firm jump on the idea?

Many companies shy away from using obvious ideas like a *bull* and *bullish* for a brokerage firm. They figure since nobody is using them, the idea can't be any good.

Not true. The best ideas are obvious ideas as long as they're not used by anyone else. The reason is obvious, too.

Obvious ideas are ideas that already exist in many consumers' minds, so a company doesn't have to have an enormous budget to introduce something new and different.

They just have to stake a claim on what's already there.

Perhaps the most effective political slogan ever written was conceived by Saatchi & Saatchi in 1979 on behalf of the Conservative party before a general election in the United Kingdom.

Incredibly effective, but also as simple as any slogan ever devised.

In the 1979 U.K. election, Conservatives led by Margaret Thatcher faced the Labour party led by James Callaghan.

Saachi & Saachi ran billboards depicting a winding line of people waiting at an unemployment office.

The 1979 U.K. election resulted in a 5.2 percent shift from Labour to the Conservatives, the largest shift since a 1945 election held after the end of World War II.

(This was the first of four consecutive elections won by Thatcher and her Conservative party.)

And what was Labour's slogan? *The better way.*

The better way is typical of many company and political slogans. It's too broad, too encompassing, too general. To drill into a mind, you need something specific, tangible and simple.

And if at all possible, use a double-entendre. *Labour isn't working.* People aren't working because the Labour party isn't working.

JetBlue has a simple slogan: *You above all.* Because it's an airline, consumers see the obvious double-entendre connotation.

Brand names can also benefit from the use of double-entendres. But they need to be relevant to the brand.

BlackBerry is a fruit and a company brand. Apple is also a fruit and a company brand. Both are good names because they are unique, but they don't benefit from their association with their fruits.

On the other hand, here are three double-entendre brand names that do benefit from their dual associations.

Blockbuster is an attribute attributed to a motion picture that turns out to be a big hit.

Hence the association with Blockbuster Video, a retail store that rents *blockbuster* movies.

In the mind, *Wearhouse* is also *Warehouse,* an attribute associated with a large store that sells merchandise at low prices.

The double-entendre communicates the idea that *Men's Wearhouse* is a very large store selling men's clothing at inexpensive prices.

Staples, an office superstore, is a word with two additional meanings. (1) *Staples* are basic supplies, and (2) *Staples* are metal prongs used in staplers. (The "L" in the *Staples* logotype is bent to symbolize a staple.)

The additional meanings contribute to the association of the *Staples* brand name with "supplies for businesses."

That doesn't sound like much, but consider this. Business people don't start by thinking, What can I buy from *Staples?*

They start by thinking, I need paper and pens and other supplies. Where should I go to buy them?

Office Depot sounds like a train station and *OfficeMax* sounds like a business on steroids. That leaves *Staples,* the first choice for business staples and the leader in the category.

In 2013, Office Depot merged with OfficeMax. But two losers don't make a winner. Here are sales last year.

Staples . . . . $22.5 billion.

Office Depot & OfficeMax . . . $16.1 billion.

Staples made $135 million in net profits while the combination of Office Depot and OfficeMax lost $354 million.

Life Savers is another brand that benefits from a double-entendre. More than 100 years ago, a candy maker in Garrettsville, Ohio invented a "summer candy" that can withstand heat better than chocolate.

The name was derived from its similarity to lifebuoys used for saving people fallen from boats.

Life Savers quickly became the No.1 mint-candy brand in America.

The candy is the reason that today lifebuoys and life preservers are often called *life savers.*

When your brand name is a double-entendre, you can often double its impact by developing a slogan reflects this fact. Some examples.

Tide hasn't used its double-entendre slogan for decades, but Trane and John Deere are still using theirs.

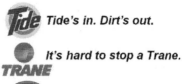

Tide's in. Dirt's out.

It's hard to stop a Trane.

Nothing runs like a Deere.

The Trane slogan is 21 years old. The John Deere slogan is something like 75 years old. The leaping deer on the Deere logotype is even older. It was first used on a John Deere logotype 140 years ago.

Double-entendres are particularly useful in communicating ideas like low price. No brand really wants to be known as "cheap."

How could Southwest Airlines communicate low price? Here is one way to do that.

Most people know the airline serves no food on its flights. They only serve peanuts. And "peanuts"

Fly for peanuts.

is common slang for "very few dollars." Hence, the double-entendre.

Sometimes a double-entendre can actually hurt a brand.

For many years, Toyota's advertising slogan was: *Moving forward.* They obviously meant to imply the company was continually improving its line of automobiles.

But the literal meaning of the slogan can lead consumers to ask, What, is there no reverse gear on a Toyota?

Subaru, on the other hand, had a long-term double-entendre slogan that was not only was memorable, but also managed to communicate two important benefits. *Inexpensive and built to stay that way.*

What is Subaru's current slogan? Unless you are a Subaru owner, you are unlikely to have any idea. *Confidence in motion.*

This is so typical of today's slogans. They're short because they're designed as taglines which makes it difficult to use reversal, repetition and other memory-enhancing techniques.

Some of the best advertising slogans use combinations of techniques that can greatly increase their effectiveness.

Roto-Rooter's slogan is a rhyme, but *troubles* is a double-entendre. *Away go troubles down the drain.*

The best surprise is no surprise combines repetition and reversal.

Borrowing ideas from the past can also be a very good technique. During the Spanish-American War of 1898, there were two battlecries.

Remember the Maine! was the battlecry of the American troops that invaded Cuba after the sinking of the battleship USS Maine.

And *Cuba Libre!* was the battlecry of the Cuba Liberation Army fighting for the country's independence from Spain.

When the Americans invaded, they brought along Coca-Cola, their favorite soft drink.

Mixing Coke with the local Bacardi rum resulted in a drink christened by the Americans  as *Cuba Libre.* A combination of Coca-Cola, Bacardi rum and lime, the drink went on to become popular throughout Latin America.

And the company, Bacardi Limited, became the world's largest privately-held, family-owned spirits company.

After overthrowing the military dictatorship in 1959, Fidel Castro established the first communist state in the Western Hemisphere.

The following year, after nationalizing and banning private property, Castro confiscated Bacardi's Cuban assets.

Luckily, a few years prior to the revolution, Bacardi had constructed distilling plants in Puerto Rico and Mexico.

Today, Bacardi rum is the world's fifth largest-selling liquor brand and Rum & Coke, aka *Cuba Libre,* is its most-popular mixed drink.

We see this as a big opportunity for the brand. Look at the headlines of a couple of Bacardi advertisements in the past.

Bacardi white tastes great mixed because it takes great unmixed.

Bacardi rum. Sip it before you add the cola.

Instead of these insipid advertisements, the brand could focus on its most-popular drink, Rum and Coke.

"Hammer your strength" is one of the most important principles in the field of marketing. Here is what we would suggest for Bacardi.

Perhaps Bacardi Limited doesn't realize how powerful the *Cuba Libre* idea is.

Drink a Cuba Libre.

And toast the day Cuba will be free.

According to the website TheMost10.com, Rum & Coke is second to beer as the world's most-popular alcoholic beverage. (Wine is No.8.)

A double-entendre starts out with two different mental connections in the mind. And the more connections, the more memorable the idea.

A mind continues to shift back and forth between the two concepts, deepening the connections and making them unforgettable.

The creators of television shows like *Castle* and *Blue Bloods* know the power of multiple-plot lines to hold attention and create interest. Two stories are often entwined.

For example, the story of a detective solving a crime can alternate between the details of the crime itself and a potential love affair with the detective's partner.

Multiple-plot lines in television shows and motion pictures act like double-entendres in marketing.

The makers of wine also know the power of multiple "flavor notes." An expensive wine is not a single flavor, but a blend of flavors.

Here are excerpts from typical reviews for three highly-rated wines.

. . . offering citrus, vanilla and toast aromas and flavors, with intriguing notes of lime and citronella.

. . . many layers of blackberry, black olive, cherry, blueberry and clove on a smooth and elegant frame.

. . . well-focused on dark berry, plum, currant and cherry. Cedar, crushed rock and loamy earth notes emerge on the finish.

Consider soft drinks like ginger ale, lemonade and orangeade. None of these are as popular as cola.

Here is a typical list of what goes into cola: Caramel, caffeine, sugar, carbonated water, citric or phosphoric acid and eight oils (orange, lime, lemon, cassia, nutmeg, coriander, lavender and neroli.)

What does cola taste like? Multiple flavors, of course. That's why cola is by far the most-popular carbonated soft drink.

Some of the most-memorable quotations achieved their longevity with the use of double-entendres.

We must hang together or assuredly we will all hang separately. Benjamin Franklin.

Yesterday is history. Tomorrow is a mystery. And today is a gift. That's why they call it the present. Eleanor Roosevelt.

HEADLESS BODY IN TOPLESS BAR. Notorious headline from the New York Post.

Marketing Matters. A column I wrote for Nation's Restaurant News.

There's also an interesting analogy between pictures and words. A *double-envision* in pictures is similar to a *double-entendre* in words.

Most pictures have a single point of interest. And most words and phrases have a single meaning.

But a *double-envision* has two major points of interest.

With two points of interest, this poster for the movie "Jaws" forces the viewer's eyes to shift from the swimmer to the shark's jaws. And back again. A double seeing, or a *double-envision.*

Double-entendres work the same way. The two meanings oscillate back and forth deepening the overall impression in your mind.

It's the same trick you can use to remember the name of someone you have just met. Let's say his name is Bob. Just think of someone else who is also named "Bob." Then associate each name with an attribute.

Let's say the well-known Bob is tall and the Bob you just met is short.

Now the name "Bob" in your mind is a double entendre. One short Bob and one tall Bob.

Double-entendres can be useful in developing brand names.

In the year 1994, Jeff Bezos launched an Internet site to sell books. His original name was Cadabra.com, but he soon changed the name because it sounded too much like the word "cadaver."

Jeff Bezos new name, Amazon.com, was an excellent choice because it was a double-entendre.

Earth's biggest bookstore.

Amazon: Earth's biggest river and *Earth's biggest bookstore.*

Today, Amazon.com is worth $248 billion on the stock market.

(If he had used Cadabra name, I wonder how much the company would be worth on the stock market.)

In the year 2001, Mark Duffey created a revolutionary new concept called a "funeral-concierge" service.

He set out to simplify and streamline the funeral-planning process by offering end-of-life planning services. Both as an advance planning option or at the time of need.

But what brand name might be appropriate for such a service?

When it comes to death, most people shy away from explicit words. Nobody ever dies. They just pass away.

Then, too, what visual hammer could a funeral-planning company use in a logotype?

Again, a double-entendre solved both problems.

The first nationwide funeral planning and concierge service.

Everest, or *Ever rest,* became both the brand name and the trademark.

Everest funeral-concierge service has become quite successful. Currently, the Everest company has more than 25 million participants.

Chapter 10

CREATING A SLOGAN

Let's say there was a slogan department in your advertising agency or marketing organization and someone handed you a briefing.

"Here's the name, the pricing, the distribution and the position. Now it's your turn to come up with a catchy slogan."

What do you do next? Blow a whistle and call time out.

As a marketing principle, nothing is fixed until everything is fixed. A company should consider all the elements of a marketing program "up for grabs" until it can develop a unified strategy, including a slogan.

The place to start is with the brand name itself. Kraft Foods Group has just introduced nine meal-starters called Kraft Recipe Makers with an ad budget of $30 million.

Kraft Recipe Makers will lead consumers to assume the brand consists of recipes for using cheese in a creative way.

Not cooking sauces for making chicken cacciatore, New England pot roast and chicken enchilada.

(To further complicate things, Kraft Foods Group also recently introduced another meal-starter product line, *Kraft Fresh Take.*)

What was the slogan of *Kraft Recipe Makers?*

Get your chef together. If you say it out loud, you will notice the mildly-naughty double-entendre.

In spite of $30 million of advertising, how likely is it that consumers will associate *Get your chef together* with *Kraft Recipe Makers?*

Highly unlikely. That's the problem with line extensions of which Kraft is a serial offender.

What's the slogan of Kraft Fresh Take? *You make it fresh.*

With a name like Kraft Fresh Take, why in the world would you want to have a slogan that adds nothing to the brand name?

That's typical thinking. What's the primary benefit of the brand? It's the idea of making the meal starter fresh? So that's the focus.

Logical thinking but foolish marketing. To be effective, slogans first have to be memorable, whether they say anything or not.

In reality, of course, it's not possible to build memorable slogans around line extensions like *Kraft Recipe Makers* and *Kraft Fresh Take.* The key word is *Kraft* and in consumers' minds, *Kraft* means *cheese.*

So to create a memorable slogan for *Kraft,* you would have to say something about cheese. Is it natural? Or organic? Or what?

And then, how would you put that idea into a memorable saying?

Another mistake companies can make is to try to establish slogans for each of their line extensions. Take *Pepsi-Cola* and *Diet Pepsi.*

How can consumers keep these two ideas separate in their minds?

And how can they remember which one is the *Pepsi* slogan and which one is the *Diet Pepsi* slogan?

Live for now. **Love every sip.**

To reduce marketing confusion, it's best to use a single slogan for each brand and forget about separate slogans for line extensions.

While not very memorable, *Open happiness* has a chance to be identified with both *Coca-Cola* and its line extension, *Diet Coke.*

Consumers don't treat Diet Coke and regular Coke as two brands. Diet Coke is just regular Coca-Cola with an artificial sweetener.

Another thing to consider is the brand's position in its category. Is it the leader, the No.2 brand or an also-ran?

The best position to own is "leadership." Let me explain.

What do consumers want? They want to buy the "better" brand. That's why favorable stories in the media and the web are so helpful, as well as favorable rankings in Consumer Reports.

But what doesn't work well are "betterness" claims in advertising. *The best-tasting pizza on the market* isn't going to drive consumers to your pizza. Years of constant advertising have convinced consumers that everybody has the better pizza or the better brand.

What does convince consumers, however, are leadership claims. If your brand is the leader, think consumers, it must be better.

That's behind the continuing success of leading brands like Hertz, Heinz and Hellmann's.

If there is confusion about which brand in a category is the leader, then it makes a lot of sense to consider using leadership claims like Oscar Mayer, Oreos and Titleist.

A leadership claim could be particularly helpful in a category where a long-time leader has lost its leadership.

Oscar Mayer *America's favorite bacon.*

OREO *Milk's favorite cookie.*

Titleist *#1 ball in golf.*

Take the car-rental category. I think you'll find that some 90 percent of car-rental customers think Hertz is the leader in rent-a-cars.

Hertz was the first car-rental company, but Hertz currently is not the category leader. Enterprise is.

Enterprise Rent-A-Car was first to open rental offices in the suburbs. When you combine its suburban business and airline-terminal business, the company is ahead of Hertz.

A leadership claim would be ideal because few consumers know that Enterprise is *The real leader in car rentals.*

We are strong believers in a concept called "focus." One reason is that a focus simplifies the development of a memorable slogan.

Take Sears, for example. What can one say about a department store that sells everything? Not much.

Here is a list of the slogans Sears has been using in the past.

Sears 2005: *The good life at a great price.*

Sears 2007: *Where it begins.*

Sears 2009: *Life. Well spent.*

Sears 2014: *Where better happens.*

Do you remember any of these? Probably not. But Sears does have a leadership position it could exploit before the position slips away. Sears is No.1 in major appliances, with 30 percent of the market.

Sears owns some powerful hard-goods brands. Sears should dump soft goods (clothing & white goods) and focus on hard goods with a slogan like: *The major seller of major appliances.*

Things are rough for Sears. Since its merger with Kmart  ten years ago, Sears has lost $3.5 billion on revenues of $435.8 billion.

Furthermore, annual sales at Sears Holdings declined every year for the last eight years in a row.

Even worse is the slow decline in Sears' share of major appliances as competitors like The Home Depot and Lowe's continue to grow their appliance market shares.

When things are going against you, you need to make a major move. Like a move into major appliances. With a leadership claim.

In truth, few companies use leadership slogans and there's a reason. Most category leaders tend to be heavily-advertised brands.

And heavily-advertised brands are also heavily-researched brands. When consumers are asked if they buy brands just because the brands are market leaders, they almost universally say "no."

No one wants to think they are mindless followers of the crowd.

They want to think of themselves as independent thinkers who decide what to buy on their own. Not to copy what others buy.

So why do consumers buy brands like Hertz, Heinz and Hellmann's? They usually say, "Because they're better."

Down inside a consumer's psyche there must be a voice whispering, People buy products they consider to be better. If a brand is the leader, it must be the better product.

If you want your brand to be known as *better*, don't tell consumers your brand is *better*. Tell consumers your brand is *the leader*.

The vast majority of brands, of course, can't be market leaders. So how can an also-ran compete with the leader?

Narrow your focus. Marketing strategy is similar to military strategy. When outnumbered, a military general concentrates his forces at a point where he can outnumber his enemy.

You can do that by focusing all your resources on a single attribute.

By focusing on *driving*, BMW went from nowhere to become the world's leading luxury-vehicle brand.

By focusing on *safety*, Volvo went from nowhere to become a very successful imported car brand.

By focusing on *shipping*, Zappos went from nowhere to become the leading Internet shoe brand.

But not any attribute. As a general rule, there is only one attribute that is going to work. But how can you discover that one attribute? By asking yourself a simple question.

What's the No.1 problem that's keeping our brand from growing? Not, What are "all" the problems we face? The brand that tries to tackle everything is going to wind up nowhere.

Take BMW. What was the No.1 problem that was keeping the brand from growing? Mercedes-Benz.

There used to be only two luxury vehicles imported from Germany. With Audi, now there are three.

Automobile buyers were already sold on German luxury vehicles, but why should they buy a BMW instead of a Mercedes-Benz?

Compare the two. Mercedes-Benz made large, comfortable vehicles. BMW made smaller, more-nimble machines.

Large, comfortable. **Smaller, more-nimble.**

This was the major difference between the two brands.

How could BMW dramatize this difference?

In 1975, BMW launched its driving campaign with an advertisement that had an immodest headline.

It's rare that you will find the problem, the solution and the slogan all wrapped up in just one headline.

No wonder BMW's slogan, *The ultimate driving machine,* lasted for more than three decades.

Take Zappos. What's the No.1 problem that is keeping the Internet shoe site from growing?

The return problem. No matter how much a consumer likes a pair of shoes, they won't buy them until they can try them on.

And what if they don't fit? Send them back, but what does that cost? Not very much. A $200 pair of dress heels can weigh less than a pound.

It's not the few dollars a return would cost that bothers consumers. It's the feeling that paying for the return is "wasted money."

Free shipping, both ways solves the problem keeping Zappos.com from growing.

Free shipping. Both ways.

Ten years after its launch, the Zappos.com website was sold to Amazon for $1.2 billion.

One thing you can't ignore in creating a slogan is your brand name. A good percentage of the time, you will need to change the brand name in order to develop an effective slogan.

There are too many brands on the market like *Kraft Recipe Makers.* (Actually, the company recently withdrew the brand from the market, presumably for poor sales.)

A potential slogan-maker first has to convince the powers-that-be that the brand needs a totally-different name.

Brands need "brand" names, not "generic" names. Oddly enough, Zappos was first called *ShoeSite* before changing its name to *Zappos,* a variation of zapatos, the Spanish word for shoes.

Think about *ShoeSite* from the point of view of word-of-mouth. Imagine a conversation between two people.

Where did you buy your shoes?

At ShoeSite.

I know. But which shoe site?

Sometime the difference between an ineffective brand name and an effective name is quite small.

Rooms, in my opinion, would be an ineffective brand name for a furniture store. *Rooms To Go,* however, has become one of the largest furniture chains in the country.

When your name is a unique combination of generic words like Rooms To Go, your slogan needs to connect with your brand name or consumers will be confused.

Rooms To Go does this in a brilliant way.

You might think, Why should Rooms To Go admit that buying the piece is only *saving a little?*

Buy the piece, save a little.
Buy the room, save a lot.

That's the classic way to create believability in a marketing message. "Admit a negative and the prospect will give you the positive."

Take the Volkswagen campaign of years ago. *Lemon* is the worst thing you could say about a car.

Yet, Volkswagen turned the word into a positive by pointing out that the *lemon* in the ad was a new car rejected for a minor fault.

And how about this 1970 VW ad bragging about how ugly the car is.

Most advertising slogans (and advertisements) are too serious.

They don't talk to consumers in words that are frank, friendly and folksy. Furthermore, they sell the category, not the brand.

A good example is Fage, the first brand of Greek yogurt introduced in the America market. Fage arrived in 1998, nine years before Chobani hit supermarket shelves.

Half the yogurt market is now Greek yogurt, but the leading brand is not Fage. It's Chobani.

Current market shares: Chobani, 47 percent. Fage, just 14 percent.

The leading producer of Greek yogurt in Greece is not Chobani, it's Fage with more than 25 percent market share. (Vivartia is No.2.)

Getting into the mind first is what builds leaders; not getting into the market first. Be honest. Did you ever hear of Greek yogurt before Chobani arrived? I didn't and most consumers probably didn't either.

And look at the Fage packages. Is *Total* the brand name?

"Fage Total Greek Yogurt" is what Fage calls its products, possibly because competitive products are not "total" Greek

yogurt. If that is so, what does Total 0% and Total 2% mean?

(Fat content, but it's an odd way to communicate a simple idea.)

The Fage approach violates the law of the category. If you want to be the category leader, you should forget about your features (thicker and creamier) and focus on your leadership credentials.

Even today, late in the game, Fage still has a chance to capture the leadership position. But it needs a new slogan.

Fage needs to compare itself with Chobani in the way that BMW compared itself with Mercedes-Benz.

Fage might consider doing something like this. Advertise the fact that Chobani might be No.1 in America, but Fage is the No.1 Greek yogurt in Greece.

No.1 Greek yogurt in America.   **No.1 Greek yogurt in Greece.**

Many companies like Fage hesitate to use a simple, clear, down-to-earth idea that defines a "position" in the marketplace. They prefer soft, mushy expressions that don't hamper their ability to be "all things to all people."

Check these ten slogans and see if you can figure out which brands have been using them.

Not so easy to do, is it?

People might remember some of these slogans, but have trouble linking them with the brands that use the slogans.

Advance.
Truth in engineering.
Life's better when we're connected.
New thinking. New possibilities.
Inspired performance.
Expect great things.
Because you're worth it.
Never stop improving.
The best or nothing.
Now that's better.

That's one of the biggest problem in creating a memorable slogan. Marketing people will spend many hours and days coming up with ideas to define their brands.

But they seldom think about connecting their slogans to the brands. They just assume advertising will do it.

For the record, here are the ten brands which use the ten slogans. Let's look at each slogan and see how it might be improved.

Advance.

The only advantage of a slogan like this one is the alliteration between the two words, *Acura* and *advance*.

But the word *advance* doesn't communicate much of anything about Acura. (Sometime you want to "advance" a vehicle, sometimes you want to "reverse" it.)

Acura needs to start with the position of the brand in the mind. What's an Acura? It was the first Japanese luxury automobile brand.

Acura made the mistake of selling both expensive and inexpensive vehicles under the Acura name.

That allowed the second Japanese luxury brand (Lexus) to establish the high-end position.

One trick is to "touch base with reality." Everyone knows that Lexus is the No.1 Japanese luxury brand.

The other Japanese luxury vehicle.

So here is how to put Acura in the same category as Lexus, using a reversal slogan.

Acura: The other Japanese luxury vehicle.

This slogan does two things: (1) It suggests to every Lexus prospect that he or she ought to consider buying an Acura, and (2) It upgrades Acura from somewhere in the "mushy middle" to the high end.

Why not *Acura: The first Japanese luxury vehicle?*

Isn't leadership the most-important aspect of a marketing program? True, but claiming to be "first" admits that Acura wasn't good enough to maintain its leadership once Lexus arrived on the market.

Truth in engineering.

Every statement implies something about the brand's competition. Audi's slogan implies that its competitors are not very truthful.

In Germany, there are three strong luxury brands: Mercedes-Benz, BMW and Audi. Consumers are unlikely to believe Audi is more truthful than either BMW or Mercedes-Benz.

That's especially so since BMW is the world's largest-selling luxury vehicle and Mercedes has a strong reputation at the high end.

But here's a surprising fact about the German luxury-vehicle market. Mercedes is the leader, but Audi outsells BMW.

In America, of course, Audi trails far behind its German rivals. Audi sales are half that of BMW and Mercedes.

The driving machine preferred in Germany.

Here is how to try to make the American market look more like the German market. *Audi: The driving machine preferred in Germany.*

122

Also, the Audi trademark (four interlocking circles) could be used in TV commercials to symbolize four wheels driving on a winding road, much like the original BMW television commercials.

This might be particularly effective since BMW seems to have shifted much of its advertising budget from television to print.

Life's better when we're connected.

Life's better for whom? Bank of America or the customer?

The slogan sounds warm and fuzzy, but sails over the prospect's head because it doesn't have a tangible relationship to a bank account.

With two specific words like *bank* and *America* in the brand name, a better strategy would be to connect the two. My thought.

Bank of America: America's biggest bank.

Reversals are particular memorable because they lock

the slogan with the name. That's the problem with most ad slogans. They have little connection with their brand names.

Years ago, a very large bank in The Netherlands decided to invade the American market. The bank was call "ING."

ING might be a good brand name in the Dutch language, but not in the English language. In America, ING is only half a word.

Change the name, we said. When that piece of advice was rejected, we offered a second solution.

The last word in bank . . . ing.

The last word in bank . . ing.

That advice was also rejected and the ING bank forged ahead with many approaches, none of which caught fire. Finally, the

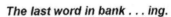

company sold its American banking operations to Capital One.

New thinking. New possibilities.

Repetition of the word "new" helps the memorability of the slogan, but doesn't connect Hyundai with automobiles.

Instead, it connotes high-tech products like computers.

Hyundai has become a successful Korean car brand at the low end. But it's making a mistake, in my opinion, by trying to move upscale with its Genesis and Equus models.

Drop the high-end models and focus on the low end is my advice. Introduce a second brand (like Toyota's Lexus or Honda's Acura) if Hyundai wants to move upscale.

Hyundai has received a lot of publicity about the upscale features in its downscale automobiles. That would make a good slogan.

High-end luxury at the low end.

Hyundai: High-end luxury at the low end.

The alliteration with Hyundai and the reversal *High end, low end* would help in creating a memorable slogan. Also, it would tie-in with the favorable publicity the brand has received.

Inspired performance.

"Inane" is an alliterative word that best describes this Infiniti slogan. Generalities like inspiration, reliability, high-quality, low-maintenance are not good working materials for an advertising slogan.

Sales are also inane. (Less than half of Lexus.) Infiniti needs to do what Avis did years ago. Present itself as an alternative.

But, of course, that's also what Acura needs to do. They both could use the same slogan. And whoever does it first will pre-empt the idea.

Infiniti: The other Japanese luxury vehicle.

The other Japanese luxury vehicle.

Put yourself in a buyer's shoes. Automobiles, smartphones, watches and other items are "badge" brands.

They tell friends and relatives where you are in the hierarchy of life. If you buy an Infiniti vehicle, you want to be perceived as a successful, upscale individual.

But what if consumers don't know that Infiniti is a luxury vehicle? That's what concerns potential Infiniti buyers. (After all, toll lanes are *Lexus lanes*, not *Infiniti lanes*.)

Positioning Infiniti as a luxury vehicle will reassure potential buyers they are getting a luxury badge.

There's another angle. The best advertising slogans are "involving." *The other Japanese luxury vehicle* encourages consumers to find out, What's the difference between a Lexus and an Infiniti?

To increase sales, that's exactly what Infiniti should be talking about. The difference between a Lexus and an Infiniti.

Expect great things.

No alliteration, no rhyme, no reversals, no repetition, no double-entendre. My mother has been a shopper at Kohl's for at least a decade and couldn't tell me what the brand's slogan is.

Killer clothes at painless prices.

What's a Kohl's? A store selling designer clothing at bargain prices. My suggestion for a slogan: *Kohl's: Killer clothes at painless prices.*

Two alliterations and one reversal *(killer* and *painless)* help make the slogan memorable.

Because you're worth it.

This slogan of the French cosmetic company is now 43 years old. It's also psychologically sound because it communicates and justifies the higher cost of L'Oreál cosmetics.

I wouldn't change it, with one caveat. I wonder how many women associate *Because you're worth it* with L'Oreál?

Leading cosmetic in France.

If this percentage is not high, then I would change the slogan. Here is one possibility. *L'Oreál: Leading cosmetic in France.*

Since L'Oreál's biggest competitor in America is Olay, the slogan hammers the most-significant difference between the two brands.

Never stop improving.

This Lowe's slogan is an "insider" slogan. Since The Home Depot and Lowe's are "home improvement warehouses," *Never stop improving* is a double-entendre on the concept of "improvement."

Trouble is, how many consumers call Lowe's and The Home Depot home improvement warehouses? Not very many.

When only two brands dominate a category, the problem is clear-cut. The No.1 brand should promote leadership, but the No.2 brand should promote one singular difference.

Coca-Cola is the old, established, authentic cola, *The real thing.* Your parents drank Coke, so Pepsi-Cola focused on the youth market with the slogan: *The Pepsi Generation.*

McDonald's is the leading hamburger chain, so Burger King focused on the way it prepared its burgers: *Broiling, not frying.*

The Home Depot is messy and male-oriented, so Lowe's became neat, clean and female-oriented. It should have used that in its slogan. My suggestion: *Lowe's: Low prices the neater, cleaner way.*

Retail chains today are under constant pressure from Internet stores that often sell merchandise for rock-bottom prices.

Low prices the neater, cleaner way.

Alliteration of *Lowe's* and *low* helps the chain communicate its low-price position in competition with Home Depot and Internet stores.

The best or nothing.

There's something snobbish about this slogan. If you can't come up with the money to buy a Mercedes-Benz automobile, you should walk or maybe buy a bicycle.

Furthermore, the slogan doesn't state a reason for being the "best." I would recommend that Mercedes-Benz go back to a slogan it had been using a number of years ago.

Mercedes-Benz: Engineered like no other car in the world.

Engineered like no other car in the world.

Mercedes is known as a German vehicle and Germany is known for "engineering," so the slogan has believability, a key ingredient in any effective slogan. In essence, the engineering slogan tells consumers "why" Mercedes-Benz is the best.

Now that's better.

Because Wendy's is often compared to McDonald's and Burger King, the slogan makes sense. The chain has created the perception that it is "a cut above" the other two.

Now that's better, however, sounds like what you might say to a child after putting a Band-Aid on a cut. Why not say it directly?

Wendy's: A cut above the others. This slogan might be particularly effective in today's fast-food environment.

A cut above the others.

One of the newest ideas is the "better burger" chain: Five Guys, Smashburger, Shake Shack and a number of other chains.

They are educating consumers about the benefits of better burgers. But there is a downside to Five Guys and Smashburger. They are slower and more expensive than the three traditional burger chains.

So the idea of *A cut above the others* might encourage consumers to switch to Wendy's from McDonald's and Burger King.

And, of course, *A cut* is also a double-entendre for a cut of meat and a position in the marketplace.

One more thing: A visual.

But there's one more thing you should consider. A visual to help you communicate your slogan. A powerful battlecry needs both.

Chapter 11

VISUAL HAMMER

Creating a slogan is only half the battle. The other half of the battle is a visual that will help drive your slogan into prospects' minds.

The contour bottle helps drive *The real thing* into the minds of cola drinkers.

The cowboy helps drive the *masculinity* of Marlboro cigarettes into smokers' minds.

The straw-in-the-orange helps drive *Not from concentrate* into the minds of Tropicana prospects.

Even *The ultimate driving machine* would not have been effective, in my opinion, without a visual hammer.

And what was BMW's visual hammer? It was television commercials showing BMWs being driven by happy owners over winding roads.

Over the years, there have been many, many advertising campaigns showing beautiful automobiles being driven over lush, winding roads. Even today, you see the same images in many car commercials.

The hammers are terrific, but the nails are missing.

The trick is to find the right combination of a visual hammer and a verbal nail.

When these two work together, as they did for BMW, you have a potentially powerful battlecry.

Almost every brand has a verbal slogan, but very few brands have what I have been calling a *visual hammer.*

This is true in spite of the fact that advertising is a visually-oriented profession. *A picture is worth 1,000 words,* Confucius' famous saying, has been quoted endlessly in advertising circles.

While virtually every advertising campaign is loaded with visuals, few qualify as hammers.

What's a visual hammer? It's a visual that hammers a verbal nail into consumers' minds.

One question you might be asking yourself, What's more important, the words or the pictures?

That question is like asking What's more crucial in building a house, the hammer or the nail? Both have to work together.

Marlboro's success demonstrates the power of the right combination of visual and verbal. Launched in the American market in the year 1953, Marlboro eventually became the world's largest-selling cigarette brand.

Wow! The Marlboro cowboy must be exceptionally powerful.

That's not necessarily true. That's not how advertising works. The Marlboro cowboy is only a hammer.

What was the cowboy hammer trying to do? The year Marlboro was introduced, virtually all cigarettes were "unisex" brands, appealing to both men and women.

Marlboro was conceived as a "masculine" cigarette, the first brand to focus entirely on men. (In six decades, there has never been a woman in a Marlboro ad.)

The cowboy hammer was designed to drive this "masculine" idea into smokers' minds. It was this visual/verbal combination that built the powerful Marlboro brand.

To be effective, a visual hammer also needs an element of "shock."

When it was launched, the Marlboro cowboy was a departure from the elegantly-dressed men and women smoking competitive brands.

Someone once said that a good picture might be a line of marines standing at attention and in perfect order.

A great picture, however, might be that same line of marines with a pigeon sitting on the shoulder of one of the marines.

The pigeon provides the shock that captures the viewer's attention, in the same way that the lime on top of the bottle provides the shock that made Corona the largest-selling imported beer in America.

The entire Corona advertising campaign is built around the lime on top of the bottle.

Visuals have an emotional impact that words do not.

When Tropicana dropped its straw-in-the-orange visual, consumers reacted instantly and bitterly, forcing the company to bring back the original package design.

Nobody complained that Tropicana had also changed its slogan from *Not from concentrate* to *Squeeze.*

Change a slogan and consumers will ignore you. Change a visual and consumers will bombard you with complaints.

Everywhere you look today, you will see examples of visual hammers. Thanks to its purple pill, Nexium is the third largest-selling prescription drug in America with sales last year of $6.2 billion.

Thanks to its polo player, Ralph Lauren is one of America's largest fashion brands with sales last year of $6.9 billion.

Before launching the duck, Aflac's name recognition was 12 percent. Today, it's 94 percent. These and other combinations of visual hammers and verbal nails are creating powerful brands.

Yet, today, too many slogans are like this slogan for Serta mattresses. They might make sense in the boardroom, but not in consumers' minds.

Serta: We make the world's best mattress.

No rhyme, no alliteration, no repetition, no reversal and no double-entendre.

Also, no Serta visual hammer.

As a result, the slogan has little memorability and little believability.

There must be a better way to create a memorable slogan.

And there is. You just read about it.

About the Author

LAURA RIES

Laura Ries is a leading marketing strategist, best-selling author and television personality. Together with Al Ries, the father of positioning and also her father, she consults with companies around the world.

She is co-author of five marketing books that have become bestsellers. *The 22 Immutable Laws of Branding* (1998), *The 11 Immutable Laws of Internet Branding* (2000), *The Fall of Advertising & the Rise of PR* (2002), *The Origin of Brands* (2004), and *War in the Boardroom* (2009).

Visual Hammer was Laura's debut solo book. It has been translated into the Chinese, Russian, Turkish, Polish and German languages.

Battlecry complements *Visual Hammer* by outlining five strategies for improving the effectiveness of a company's slogan or tagline.

In addition to her consulting assignments, Laura is a frequent guest on major television programs from the O'Reilly Factor to Squawk Box. She appears regularly on Fox News, Fox Business, CNBC, CNN and HLN.

And she is frequently quoted by the Associated Press, Bloomberg News and The Wall Street Journal.

A resident of Atlanta, Georgia, Laura enjoys many outdoor activities such as horseback riding, swimming, tennis, skiing and triathlons.

Her website is: LauraRies.com. Her company's website is: Ries.com.

Connect with Laura Ries

Ries & Ries consulting: ries.com
About me: lauraries.com
Blog: riespieces.com
Videos: riesreport.com
Twitter: @lauraries
Facebook: facebook.com/lauraries
LinkedIn: linkedin.com/in/lauraries
YouTube: youtube.com/user/riesreport
Instagram: instagram.com/lauraries

63079096R00077

Made in the USA
Lexington, KY
26 April 2017